tree of Life

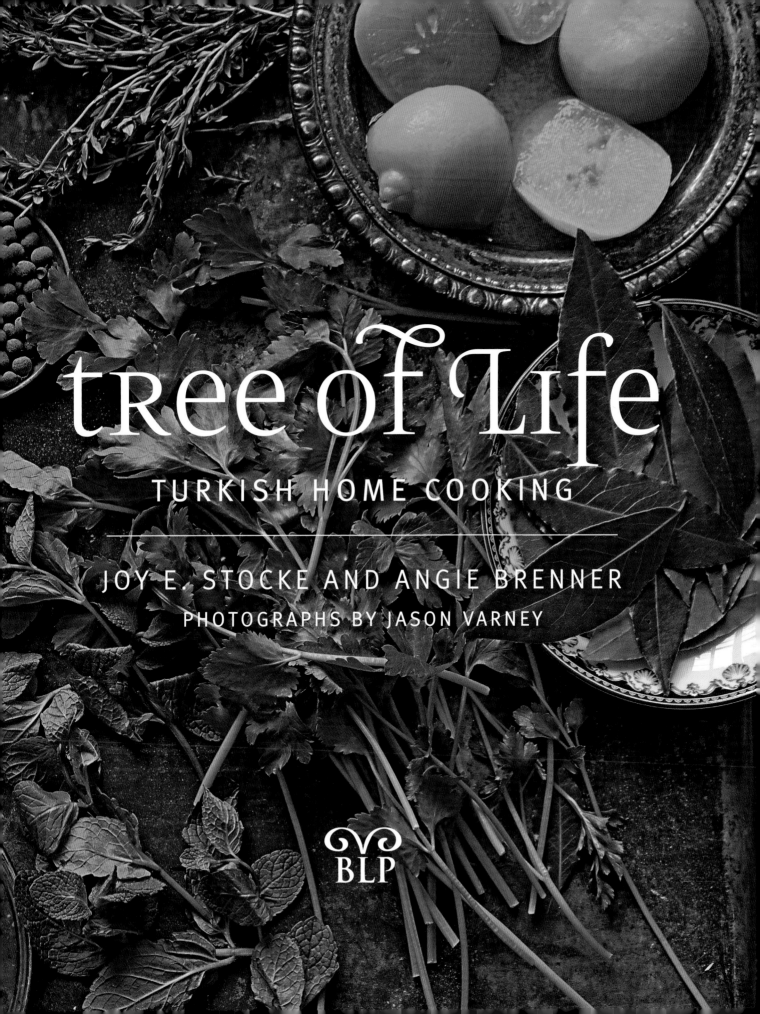

tree of Life

TURKISH HOME COOKING

JOY E. STOCKE AND ANGIE BRENNER

PHOTOGRAPHS BY JASON VARNEY

BLP

For my mother, Elizabeth Pauline, and sister, Loretta: inspiring home cooks—A.B.

For Grandma Grete and her daughter Dorothea, my mother: generous cooks and loving teachers—J.E.S.

Copyright © 2017 by Joy E. Stocke and Angie Brenner

Published in 2017 by Burgess Lea Press, a member of Quarto Publishing Group USA Inc., 400 First Avenue North, Suite 400, Minneapolis, MN 55401 USA.

Telephone: (612) 344-8100
Fax: (612) 344-8692

quartoknows.com
Visit our blogs at quartoknows.com

Burgess Lea Press titles are also available at discounts in bulk quantity for industrial or sales-promotional use. For details contact the Special Sales Manager at Quarto Publishing Group USA Inc., 400 First Avenue North, Suite 400, Minneapolis, MN 55401 USA.

10 9 8 7 6 5 4 3 2 1

ISBN 978-0-9972113-0-6

Library of Congress Control Number: 2016958544

Design Alastair Campbell
Art direction Ken Newbaker
Photography Jason Varney
Food styling Carrie Purcell
Prop styling Kristi Hunter
Production Victor Cataldo

Printed in China

Burgess Lea Press donates 100% of after-tax publishing profits on each book to culinary education, feeding the hungry, farmland preservation and other food-related causes.

contents

INTRODUCTION
tree of Life

Hoşgeldiniz. Welcome.

two thousand years before scribes recorded the story of Adam and Eve's arrival in the Garden of Eden, a myth was told throughout Mesopotamia of a garden where a divine tree grew whose branches marked the boundaries of paradise. A man and woman were placed there to guard the tree. In that garden, the couple had everything they needed at their fingertips, fruits and vegetables and herbs and flowers.

In Turkish, the divine tree, from which all life grows, is called *Ağaç Ana*, the mother tree. And with eight separate growing zones, you could say Turkey is a food-lover's Eden. For the many faiths in Anatolia—including Zoroastrian, Judaic, Christian and Islamic—the tree of life's abundance was transformed by the children of Adam and Eve into crops such as wheat, chickpeas, grapes and pomegranates. In a country blessed with fertile soil and water—the Tigris and Euphrates rivers originate in Turkey—when a Turk has access to even the smallest plot of land, he or she will grow everything from greens and herbs to fruit- and nut-bearing vines and trees.

It's been more than twenty-five years since we began our journey through the kitchens and restaurants of Anatolian friends in both Turkey and the United States, friends who have lovingly shown us how to prepare dishes that not only nourish our bodies but our hearts and memories as well. We set off in search of history, culture and art, but the most tangible evidence of our great adventure is the recipes we learned along the way—the same ones we now cook every day at home.

From the forests of northern Turkey along the Black Sea where cherries and hazelnuts grow, to the Mediterranean coast where lemon, orange and walnut trees grace fields and hillsides, we have been the lucky recipients of cooking lessons in all kinds of kitchens, some impromptu demonstrations outdoors over an open fire, and others in the grand palaces of Istanbul.

We can't imagine a better way to share these Turkish-inspired recipes than by inviting you into the kitchen. We'll lend an apron and a knife so you can chop garlic and cucumbers for the classic yogurt sauce *caçık*, or mix bulgur wheat with onions, dill, basil and mint for pilaf while we prepare chicken bought from a neighbor's farm, infusing it with cumin and preserved lemon before tucking it into the oven.

Aromas fill the kitchen, at once familiar and exotic: the tangy sweet scent of *nar ekşisi* (pomegranate molasses), hints of dried mint, lemon and Aleppo pepper mingling with pan juices of the now-golden roast chicken. We roll dough until it becomes a translucent sheet to be cut into squares for juicy lamb-stuffed *manti*, ravioli's Anatolian cousin, and stir rice flour and rosewater into simmering milk until creamy pudding coats the spoon.

Our love affair with Anatolian cooking has, at first glance, an unlikely beginning. We grew up in the American Midwest—Angie in Michigan and Joy in Wisconsin—cooking at the knees of grandmothers, mothers and aunts. The dishes these women prepared when family and neighbors gathered for Sunday dinners and holidays—often with vegetables grown in their own gardens, eggs and milk delivered to their doors and roasts from the local butcher—became a connection to the "old world" of Europe. In an era when children were still expected to be seen and not heard, we listened, absorbing accents and dialects, hearing family stories and learning recipes retold through the generations.

We left the Midwest in our teens. Angie moved to southern California, where the light, landscape and flavors of a Mediterranean climate—lemon, olive oil, bay leaf and oregano—captivated her. Joy and her family moved east to New Jersey. There, she met a friend whose Greek mother's family had emigrated from the Princes' Islands in Istanbul and who introduced her to

Anatolia comes from the Greek word *anatolé* meaning east, the land of the rising sun. Once the name of Asia Minor, today Anatolia refers to the country called Turkey, whose borders stretch from Greece and the Balkans to Armenia, Georgia, Iran, Iraq and Syria.

herb-infused roast lamb and flaky baklava.

We like to call it kismet—our destiny—when, through a mutual friend, we met for the first time in 1997 on the balcony of a pension in Kalkan, a village on Turkey's Turquoise Coast. As the setting sun turned the sea rose-pink, we—Joy, a journalist, married with a daughter, and Angie, single, a travel writer and bookstore owner—drank wine from Çanakkale (Gallipoli), bonding over a shared passion for adventure, travel and local foodways.

We'd both fallen in love with the social aspect of Turkish dining, where, in restaurants, kitchens and at dinner tables, the ingredients of a dish and its provenance are an important part of the conversation, and a dish's nuanced flavors are discussed as vigorously as the latest political scandal.

Through those lively debates, we began to see connections between familiar foods and those that took us by surprise. For instance, we learned how red chili peppers journeyed from the Americas with Spanish and Portuguese explorers and took root in Ottoman Anatolia to become Aleppo pepper, one of the world's great spices, which takes its name from the city in what is today Syria. We had always planned to visit Aleppo's medieval spice markets, but now, trusting in the resilience of the Syrian people, we can only hope for peace to return to the region and for the cherished pepper plants to grow again in the fields.

In glorious Istanbul, we embraced *meze* culture: the gathering of friends in bars and cafes over appetizers—crisp *börek* filled with spinach; plump marinated olives; creamy eggplant dip; slices of white cheese and ripe melon—served with thimbles of the anise-flavored spirit called rakı to stimulate appetite and conversation.

You could say we traveled across Turkey kitchen by kitchen and returned home with well-worn backpacks and notebooks full of recipes from people whose faces we will never forget. In fact, our own kitchens became a refuge during the years we wrote our memoir, *Anatolian Days & Nights: A Love Affair with Turkey, Land of Dervishes, Goddesses, and Saints*. Often the keenest insights would come while one of us prepared a shepherd's salad, lentil soup or kebabs after a long day of writing.

We've adapted many of these recipes brought home as souvenirs of our Anatolian journeys to make them a bit more streamlined, and to use available ingredients whenever possible. But we also encourage you to try the more detailed recipes, since they can be broken down into make-ahead steps. Better yet, invite people to cook with you and your pleasure will multiply as the kitchen fills with talk and laughter and even a tear or two—maybe from the onions, or maybe not.

Preparation becomes celebration with friends peeling eggplants for a traditional casserole or marinating lamb chops in pomegranate essence. The atmosphere warms as meat sizzles in fragrant juices and we spoon marinated olives into a bowl, setting them beside an Anatolian-inspired version of classic gougères, or pâte à choux cheese puffs, made with feta and flecked with mint, nigella seeds and Aleppo pepper. They're a touchstone from childhood when our mothers cooked their way through Julia Child, but we've made them our own with spices encountered on our grand adventure.

Gougères are best enjoyed when still warm from the oven, so ... Hanging up our aprons, we pour ourselves thimbles of rakı. "Şerefe, cheers," we say, clinking glasses.

Welcome to our kitchens.

mezes

THIS BEING HUMAN IS A GUEST HOUSE.
EVERY MORNING A NEW ARRIVAL.
—*JALALUDDIN RUMI*

small plates, vast flavors

from our first visit to Anatolia, we were captivated by the tradition of the meze table, an array of small plates of marinated olives, spicy chickpeas, pickles, seasoned nuts, firm white cheeses, hummus, stuffed grape leaves, rich eggplant puree and other savory snacks, often accompanied by anise-flavored rakı or a glass of wine. Seafood meze may include fried small fish, grilled sardines, stuffed mussels, *taramasalata* and octopus salad. We've enjoyed mezes in settings as diverse as a seaside restaurant in Istanbul's Ortaköy neighborhood while ships glided through the Bosporus toward the Sea of Marmara, and on the living room carpet of a small apartment in the central Anatolian village of Konya.

While every culture in the Middle and Near East has its own version, the Turkish meze table first gained popularity in the court of the Ottoman Empire, where complementary dishes were chosen not just to sate the appetites of the sultan and his court but also to prolong the enjoyment of an evening. We've embraced the meze table in our own homes because it's a casual, fluid way to entertain that allows us to spend time with our guests.

The list of possible mezes is diverse, from quick Turkish pickles in lemon brine and a handful of spicy chickpeas to a substantial dish like Swordfish with Lemon, Fennel and Rakı (page 156) served in appetizer portions. For our Meze Fridays (sometimes held on Saturdays), we enlist friends to keep a watchful eye on roasting peppers or help us roll out dough for Grilled Flatbread (page 58) to accompany the dips and sauces we love to make. No matter what we serve, we know the conversation will be lively and more often than not, as is common in Turkey, about food.

Afiyet olsun. Enjoy.

attila's olives with garlic and preserved lemon

MAKES 2 CUPS (310 g)

We met Attila the summer we ran a pension in Kalkan where many nights we found ourselves on the back porch at his home—a former Greek fisherman's house built of now-crumbling stone—in the center of town, known affectionately as the Ruins. Under the porch's sagging thatched roof, we'd sip rakı until dawn while Attila served his latest batch of olives, purchased from a village farmer and marinated in oil, garlic, green peppercorns and preserved lemon. Unless we're in Turkey where the black Gemlik variety is common, especially as a breakfast olive, our favorite mix to use is a blend of plump kalamatas, meaty manzanillas and nutty picholines.

2 cups (310 g) mixed olives in brine

4 large cloves garlic, peeled and lightly crushed

½ teaspoon whole green or black peppercorns

1 teaspoon thinly sliced rind from preserved lemons, or 1 tablespoon zest from a fresh lemon

1 teaspoon Aleppo pepper

Put the olives and brine in a small bowl. Add the garlic, peppercorns, preserved lemon rind, and Aleppo pepper. Gently stir to combine. Cover and marinate for at least 1 hour, turning occasionally to distribute the flavors. Olives may be stored in a covered container for up to 1 month in the refrigerator.

cucumber pomegranate pickles

SERVES 4 TO 6

1 large cucumber

½ cup (120 ml) apple cider vinegar

2 teaspoons pomegranate molasses

½ to 1 teaspoon kosher salt

⅛ teaspoon freshly ground black pepper

1 teaspoon sugar

1 tablespoon olive oil

Shops throughout Turkey called *tursulari* display jars of pickled vegetables and fruits: whole lemons, bright red peppers, long green beans, tan crescents of garlic clove layered with cherry tomatoes and tiny gherkins. This Turkish twist on marinated cucumbers has a subtle tang from pomegranate molasses. In addition to the meze table, these tart-sweet pickles go well with köfte and in green salads. The cucumber gets softer over time, so it is best to serve these within two days.

Peel the cucumber in stripes, leaving some of the green skin. Slice into 1-inch (6-cm) thick rounds and put in a shallow bowl.

In a medium bowl, combine the vinegar and pomegranate molasses and stir to blend. Add the salt, pepper and sugar. Whisk in the olive oil. Adjust seasonings to taste.

Pour the vinegar mixture over the cucumber slices and toss to combine. Refrigerate at least 30 minutes and up to 1 hour to allow the cucumbers to absorb the flavors.

savory spiced chickpeas

MAKES 3½ CUPS (770 g)

3 ½ cups (770 g) cooked chickpeas, or 2 (15-ounce/425-g) cans chickpeas, rinsed and drained
1 tablespoon olive oil
1 teaspoon kosher salt
1 teaspoon Aleppo pepper
1 teaspoon dried mint
1 teaspoon sweet paprika
1 teaspoon ground dried lemon peel

Spiced, roasted chickpeas, called *leblebi*, have been part of the Turkish meze table since at least the twelfth century. They are also a staple throughout the Levant and the Middle East. Remains of domesticated chickpeas have been found in the Neolithic city of Çayönü in southeastern Turkey on a tributary of the Tigris River. In 1875, Ottoman-Armenian composer Dikran Tchouhadjian composed a famous operetta, *The Leblebi Vendor*, dedicated to the spiced, roasted chickpea sellers whose carts were once plentiful on the streets of Istanbul.

Heat the oven to 350°F (175°C). Line a baking sheet with parchment or a Silpat.

Pat the chickpeas dry on a clean kitchen towel. Put in a medium bowl and add the olive oil to coat.

In a small bowl, combine the salt, Aleppo pepper, dried mint, sweet paprika and lemon peel. Add the spice mixture to the chickpeas, stirring gently to coat.

Spread the chickpeas on the baking sheet in a single layer and bake for 1 hour, or until they are crisp, turning them once or twice. Serve at room temperature or store in the pantry in a sealed container for up to 1 week.

The Gulf of Fethiye in the ancient Lycian capitol of Telmessos, home of King Croesus

LYCIAN DAYS

How easy it is to fall in love with Turkey's Mediterranean coast. Light shines from sea to rock in elusive reflections. Pine-covered cliffs reveal fissures and coves where fragrant boughs brush against water. From a plateau rises a four-thousand-year-old village of tombs, all that remains of the goddess-worshipping Lycians who settled in the fertile, protected valleys.

Today, our boat shelters in a bay where Phoenician traders once dropped anchor, and where we find the ruins of an ancient city glimmering beneath turquoise water. We climb over rocks onto the shore and see a girl standing in a grove of olive trees. Her hair is wrapped in a scarf edged with tiny shells and tied at the crown of her head.

She gathers olives that have fallen to the ground and studies us, two women in sunglasses, shorts and hiking boots. Gravely, she places a handful of the bitter, green fruit on a stone ledge, an offering. And then she darts away.

anatolian nut mix

MAKES 3 CUPS (385 g)

1 teaspoon Aleppo pepper

1 teaspoon kosher salt

1 teaspoon dried mint

1 tablespoon butter

1 cup (120 g) whole raw walnuts

1 cup (130 g) raw shelled pistachios

1 cup (135 g) hazelnuts or 1 cup
    (120 g) cashews

When we grow nostalgic about our travels through Anatolia, we invite friends to Meze Fridays. Austin, a regular visitor to our kitchen, is in charge of roasting the nuts, patiently turning and stirring them in an old cast-iron skillet to achieve that spice-crusted perfection. This combination of walnuts from the Aegean, pistachios from the southeast and hazelnuts from the Black Sea is a favorite. Dried mint adds a bright note, and Aleppo pepper a warm kick. If you wish, toss 1 cup (220 g) of Savory Spiced Chickpeas (page 16) into the mix. Serve warm as part of a meze platter, or with a glass of rakı or ouzo poured over ice with water.

In a small bowl, combine the Aleppo pepper, salt and dried mint.

Melt the butter in a large cast-iron or other heavy skillet over medium heat. Add the walnuts, pistachios and hazelnuts or cashews. Mix to coat the nuts with the butter.

Turn the heat to low. Sprinkle the spice mixture over the nuts and stir so that they are evenly coated.

Toast the nuts, stirring occasionally, until they are evenly browned and the spices are fragrant, about 10 minutes. Remove from the heat, stir the nuts again and let them cool in the pan. They will continue to crisp as they cool.

Once completely cooled, store the nuts in a sealed container. They will stay fresh for 2 weeks on the counter and 6 months in the refrigerator. To refresh the nuts before serving, heat them in a pan over low heat for 5 minutes.

quick saltwater and lemon pickles

SERVES 8 TO 12 AS AN APPETIZER

from our first bite in a taverna overlooking a sweep of turquoise-blue water, we were hooked on saltwater and lemon pickles. Ridiculously simple to make, this take on a classic relish tray—carrot, celery, cucumber sticks—pleases everyone. For a softer pickle, prepare up to 24 hours in advance and let the vegetables marinate in the refrigerator. For crunchier pickles, make them just before serving. For parties, we like to serve the pickles in small mason jars filled halfway with the brine. Traditionally eaten with rakı, they are perfect with cocktails.

Fennel tastes great but will impart a pronounced licorice flavor to all the vegetables. The fennel can also be brined and served separately or added to the mix. Radishes make a flavorful addition; red radishes, however, will turn the brine pink, so they too can be brined separately. The parsley turns mellow when added to the brine and makes a very compelling snack when plucked from the jar.

2 cups (473 ml) cool water

1 tablespoon kosher salt

½ cup (120 ml) lemon juice

1 tablespoon flat-leaf parsley

3 allspice berries

3 whole peppercorns

2 medium cucumbers, peeled, seeded and cut into thin 6-inch (15-cm) sticks

4 medium carrots, cut into thin 6-inch (15-cm) sticks

6 stalks celery, cut into thin 6-inch (15-cm) sticks

1 fennel bulb, sliced (optional)

1 bunch radishes, sliced in half (optional)

Put cool water into a shallow nonreactive dish. Add the salt and mix until it dissolves. Stir in the lemon juice, parsley, allspice berries and peppercorns.

Add the cucumber, carrot, celery, fennel and radishes, or divide the brine and marinate the fennel and radishes separately, according to your preference. All the vegetables should be covered with the brine.

Let the vegetables marinate for 30 minutes to 1 hour before serving. You also can make the pickles ahead of time and keep them in the refrigerator for up to 5 days. The pickles get better as they absorb more brine.

yogurt dip with cucumber and mint (çaçık)

SERVES 6 TO 8

2 cups (480 ml) plain yogurt

1 to 2 small cloves garlic, peeled

1 teaspoon kosher salt, plus more to taste

½ cup (75 g) peeled, seeded cucumber, finely diced

1 tablespoon finely chopped fresh mint, or 1 teaspoon dried mint

1 tablespoon extra-virgin olive oil, for serving

½ teaspoon Aleppo pepper, for serving

almost all cultures of greater Anatolia have a version of çaçık and the basic ingredients—yogurt, cucumber and salt—are the same. Garlic is much appreciated in Turkish çaçık and its Greek cousin, tzatziki. Herb combinations vary, but we love the cool balance of mint and garlic. For a Greek version, add dill and omit the mint and Aleppo pepper. In addition to a meze, çaçık makes an excellent sauce for fish and köfte and a protein-rich accompaniment for pilafs.

Put the yogurt in a small bowl. Place the garlic on a cutting board and sprinkle with 1 teaspoon salt. Using the side of your knife mash the garlic into a paste. Stir the garlic paste, cucumber and mint into the yogurt. Season to taste with additional salt.

Çaçık can be prepared up to a day ahead and refrigerated. To serve, spoon into a shallow bowl, drizzle with the olive oil and sprinkle with the Aleppo pepper.

baked hummus with pine nuts

SERVES 6 TO 8

Our friend Eveline, Istanbul resident and Cordon Bleu–trained chef, taught us to make her version of baked hummus at a cooking school she ran for many years in the shadow of the Blue Mosque. Spiced with cumin, blended with olive oil and a bit of yogurt to encourage the chickpea puree to puff when baked, this hummus is topped with pine nuts and melted butter infused with Aleppo pepper. Served in individual bowls with fresh hot *pide* (flatbread), this makes a lovely first course.

Heat the oven to 375°F (190°C). Pulse the garlic cloves in a food processor to mince it. Add the chickpeas, the chickpea liquid, lemon juice, olive oil, salt, white pepper and crushed cumin seeds. Pulse until the chickpeas are pureed but not gummy. Add the yogurt and pulse to blend.

Spoon the hummus into a shallow ovenproof dish and sprinkle the pine nuts over the top. Bake for 25 minutes, just until the nuts are toasted and the hummus begins to puff and brown.

While the hummus bakes, melt the butter over medium-low heat in a small skillet. Stir in the Aleppo pepper and cook for 1 minute. Keep warm.

Remove the hummus from the oven and pour the butter over the top. Serve warm with bread or crackers.

2 medium cloves garlic, peeled

3½ cups (440 g) cooked chickpeas, or 2 (15-ounce/850 g) cans chickpeas, drained, 2 tablespoons of liquid reserved

¼ cup (60 ml) lemon juice

¼ cup (60 ml) olive oil

½ teaspoon kosher salt

¼ teaspoon freshly ground white pepper

2 teaspoon crushed cumin seeds

¼ cup plain Greek yogurt

¼ cup (35 g) pine nuts

3 tablespoons butter

1 teaspoon Aleppo pepper, or ¾ teaspoon sweet paprika mixed with ½ teaspoon cayenne pepper

carrot hummus with toasted fennel seeds

MAKES 1½ CUPS (342 g)

this delicious, nourishing spread adapts the concept of hummus with familiar ingredients. It is based on *yogurtlu havuç*, a classic Turkish meze dip. Toasted fennel seeds and flaky sea salt add a bit of crunch. Serve the hummus with Classic Puffed Pide Bread (page 62) or Stuffed Flatbread (page 56).

3 large carrots, peeled and cut into chunks (about 2 cups)

1¼ teaspoons kosher salt

1 cup (236 ml) water

3 tablespoons yogurt

1 teaspoon fennel seeds

½ teaspoon flaky sea salt

Put the carrots in a medium heavy saucepan. Add the salt and 1 cup (236 ml) water.

Bring to a boil over high heat, then reduce to a simmer, stirring occasionally. Cook for 10 minutes or until the carrots are very tender and the water is nearly evaporated. If the water evaporates before the carrots are fully cooked, add a little more. Remove from the heat and drain any water left in the pan.

Add the yogurt to the carrots and blend with an immersion blender until smooth. (You can also use a food processor or blender.) The mixture should be creamy but not too thin. For a chunkier hummus, mash the carrot mixture in the pan with a fork.

In a small frying pan over medium heat, combine the fennel seeds and sea salt. Toast until the seeds are fragrant and golden brown, about 5 minutes.

Transfer the carrot hummus to a serving plate with a shallow rim. Sprinkle with the fennel salt before serving.

eggplant puree
(*patlican salatası*)

SERVES 4 TO 6

4 medium or 2 large eggplants

2 large cloves garlic, finely chopped

¼ cup (60 ml) olive oil

2 tablespoons lemon juice

1 tablespoon plain Greek yogurt

1 teaspoon kosher salt

1 teaspoon chopped flat-leaf parsley

Of the hundreds (maybe thousands) of eggplant dishes in Turkey, the puree known as *patlican* is the most iconic. The secret to making a silken, smoky puree is to roast the eggplants until their skins blacken and the flesh completely collapses. It's worth the effort to squeeze out some of the juice (which can be bitter) and remove as many seeds as possible. Serve with Grilled Flatbread (page 58), or as a side for lamb or chicken kebabs.

Heat the oven to 450°F (232°C). Line a baking sheet with foil or parchment. Poke a few holes in the eggplant and place on the prepared baking sheet.

Roast for 30 minutes or until the skins are almost blackened and the eggplants collapse. If the eggplants are large, they may need more time in the oven.

Remove the eggplants from the oven and use tongs to set them in a colander in the sink or over a bowl. Press gently on the eggplants to squeeze out some of their juice.

When cool enough to handle, set the eggplants on a cutting board. Remove and discard all of the skin. If there are a lot of seeds, remove most of them; a few seeds are fine in the finished dish.

With a sharp knife, chop the eggplant flesh as finely as possible to an almost mashed consistency. Transfer the eggplant to a bowl.

Add the garlic, olive oil, lemon juice, yogurt and salt to the eggplant and mix thoroughly. Taste and adjust seasonings. Garnish with the parsley and serve.

jeweled beet dip
(pancar çaçik)

SERVES 4 TO 6

If you were to stroll through a vegetable stall in southeastern Turkey during the second millennium BCE, you would have found beets for sale, as well as cumin. Oranges were yet to be introduced from India and China, but are now one of Turkey's top exports. We peel the beets and then grate them by hand on a box grater or in a food processor fitted with a grating disc. Serve this classic, colorful dip with Classic Puffed Pide Bread (page 62) or Grilled Flatbread (page 58).

1 heaping cup (150 g) grated beets (about 2 large or 3 medium beets)
1¼ teaspoons kosher salt, divided
½ cup (120 ml) plain Greek yogurt
1 tablespoon olive oil
½ teaspoon grated orange zest
1 tablespoon fresh orange juice
½ teaspoon ground cumin
1 teaspoon chopped flat-leaf parsley

Put the grated beets in a colander over the sink or a bowl. Sprinkle with 1 teaspoon of the salt and toss to mix well. Let the beets sit for 30 minutes, pressing on them occasionally to drain as much liquid as possible.

In a separate bowl, mix the yogurt and olive oil. Add the orange zest and juice, cumin and ¼ teaspoon salt. Mix well and set aside until the beets are fully drained.

Fold the drained beets into yogurt mixture. Spoon into a small serving bowl and garnish with chopped parsley.

sautéed mushrooms with allspice and black pepper

SERVES 4 TO 6

allspice, the main seasoning in this dish, lends sweet complexity to the earthy mushrooms. For the best flavor, buy whole allspice and grind the berries with a mortar and pestle right before using. We like to serve these warm as part of a meze selection, and they also make an excellent side dish for lamb chops.

1 pound (454 g) mushrooms (cremini, shiitake or a mixture)

3 tablespoons butter

1 tablespoon finely chopped shallots

1½ teaspoons freshly ground allspice

1 teaspoon freshly ground black pepper

½ to 1 teaspoon kosher salt, to taste

1 tablespoon lemon juice

1 tablespoon chopped flat-leaf parsley

Slice the mushrooms ½-inch (25-mm) thick, or leave whole if they are small.

Melt the butter in a medium skillet over moderate heat. Add the shallots and cook until soft but not browned. Add the allspice and cook, stirring, for 1 minute. Add the mushrooms and stir to combine.

Reduce the heat to medium-low. Cook the mushrooms for 4 to 6 minutes, until tender and nicely browned. Add a little water if the mushrooms are too dry, and to keep the allspice from becoming gritty.

Season with the pepper and salt. Remove the pan from the heat and add the lemon juice and parsley. Taste to adjust seasonings. Serve warm or at room temperature.

GRILLED HALLOUMI WITH LEMON CAPER SAUCE

SERVES 4 TO 6

One evening, in the tiny kitchen of a rented bungalow in Bellapais, a small town in northern Cyprus, we cooked thick slices of local halloumi cheese on an aluminum stovetop grate made specifically for that purpose. The salty, firm white sheep's milk cheese originated on this island in the eastern Aegean during the medieval Byzantine era. Because the fresh curd is heated before the cheese is shaped and brined, halloumi has a long shelf life and a high melting point, making it an excellent choice for the frying pan or the grill. Serve hot with Classic Puffed Pide Bread (page 62) as a salad course or as a meze with icy glasses of Persephone's Revenge (page 244).

Halloumi cheese, pride of Cyprus, turns soft and smoky on the grill.

½ cup (120 ml) olive oil

¼ cup (60 ml) lemon juice

½ teaspoon kosher salt

1 teaspoon dried oregano

1 teaspoon capers

½ pound (227 g) halloumi

Sunflower, grapeseed or canola oil, for brushing the grill

10 cherry tomatoes, halved

Freshly ground black pepper

1 teaspoon chopped parsley

Heat a grill or heat a stovetop grill pan to medium-high.

In a small saucepan, heat the olive oil over low heat until warm, but not hot. Whisk in the lemon juice, salt, oregano and capers. Remove from the heat but keep the sauce warm.

Lay the cheese on a work surface horizontally. (Halloumi comes in approximately 3 by 4-inch / 75 by 100-mm blocks.) Cut into ½-inch (13-mm) slices for a total of 8 pieces.

Brush the grill with sunflower oil. Lay the cheese slices on the grill and heat for 2 to 3 minutes, until they brown and show grill marks. Flip the cheese and grill until lightly browned, for 2 to 3 more minutes.

Put the grilled cheese on a warm platter. Scatter the tomatoes over the cheese and pour the warm dressing over it. Season with pepper and top with the parsley.

Stuffed Grape Leaves (*yaprak sarma*)

MAKES 30

The word *dolma* describes the many stuffed vegetables that exist in Turkish cuisine; any vegetable that can be hollowed, be it pepper, okra or cucumber, can be filled. *Sarma* are made by wrapping a filling in grape, cabbage or other vegetable leaves.

Preparing dolmas and sarmas has always been a communal affair. When Turkish women gather in the kitchen to stuff and roll tender leaves, they pride themselves on making the thinnest, tightest sarmas, often using an index finger to indicate that they must not be any thicker.

There are almost as many dolma and sarma fillings as there are cooks. The Ottomans added sour cherries, chickpeas, currants and pine nuts to various fillings. The combination of minced lamb, rice, cinnamon and lemon is also popular. Whether you're fortunate enough to have neighbors providing fresh leaves for blanching from their own grapevines as Angie does or you use them from a jar, the process of making sarmas becomes as much about gathering family or friends in your kitchen to stuff and roll the leaves as it is about serving this classic Turkish finger food.

Serve the sarmas warm or at room temperature with lemon wedges and plenty of Yogurt Dip with Cucumber and Mint (page 22).

FOR THE FILLING

¼ cup (35 g) dried currants or raisins

3 tablespoons olive oil

2 medium onions, finely chopped

2 cloves garlic, minced

2 tablespoons pine nuts or shelled pistachio nuts

¾ teaspoon ground allspice

¾ teaspoon cinnamon

1 teaspoon chopped dill

¾ teaspoon Aleppo pepper

1 tablespoon finely chopped fresh mint, or 1 teaspoon dried mint

1 teaspoon sugar

1 tablespoon tomato paste

1½ cups (270 g) basmati rice

½ teaspoon kosher salt

¼ teaspoon freshly ground black pepper

FOR ROLLING THE SARMA

30 grape leaves, fresh (see Preparing Fresh Grape Leaves, opposite) or store-bought

¾ cup (177 ml) olive oil

¼ cup (60 ml) lemon juice, or the juice from 1 medium lemon

Put the currants in a small bowl. Cover with warm water and soak for 15 minutes, draining any leftover liquid.

Heat the olive oil in a medium pot or large skillet over medium-low heat. Add the onions and garlic and cook for about 5 minutes until soft but not browned. Stir in the pine nuts, allspice, cinnamon, dill, Aleppo pepper, mint, sugar and tomato paste. Add the rice and ¾ cup (177 ml) water and bring the mixture to a boil.

Turn the heat to low. Cover and simmer until the water is absorbed and the

(RECIPE CONTINUES)

Stems are removed from the grape leaves before they're rolled into rice-stuffed sarmas.

PREPARING FRESH GRAPE LEAVES

Pick about 30 grape leaves from the vine up to 1 day before you want to make the sarmas. Look for unblemished medium to large leaves of similar size. Cut off any stems. Wash the leaves thoroughly. If picking the leaves ahead, wrap them in paper towels and place in a plastic bag. Keep in the refrigerator until ready to use.

To blanch the leaves, bring a large pot of water to a rapid boil. Using tongs, drop 2 to 3 leaves into the pot at a time, and boil until soft and pliable. Young leaves in the spring will take only about 30 seconds. If the leaves are harvested in late summer or fall, they may take up to 1 minute.

Carefully remove the leaves and lay them on a work surface, shiny side down, with the wide part of the base facing you.

Preparing stuffed grape leaves has always been a communal affair.

rice is still chewy, 10 to 15 minutes. (The rice will continue to cook inside the sarmas.)

Remove the pot from the heat and add the salt and pepper, adjusting to taste. Stir in the currants, if using. Set the filling aside to cool. The filling can be made a day ahead and refrigerated.

If using fresh grape leaves, prepare according to the instructions on page 31. If using grape leaves from a jar or can, gently rinse them to remove excess salt. Trim the stems to the base of the leaf if necessary.

To make the sarmas, separate the grapes leaves and place a leaf on a clean work surface, shiny side down, with the wide base of the leaf nearest you. Put 1 teaspoon of filling at the base of the leaf. (You can adjust the amount of filling

depending on the size of the leaf, but do not overfill. Overfilling the leaves will cause the sarmas to burst during cooking.)

Fold the sides of the leaves inward, right side first and left side over right, covering the filling. Begin rolling the leaf from the base toward the top, continually tucking in the sides of the leaf to make a tight cigar shape. Repeat until all the leaves have been filled.

To cook the sarmas, invert a heatproof ceramic plate in the bottom of a large pot and cover with a layer of grape leaves, or use a steamer basket lined with grape leaves so that the sarmas do not sit directly on the bottom of the pan. Carefully place the sarmas on the plate, seam-side down and very close together in one tight layer. Stack another layer of sarmas on top as needed. A snug fit will keep them from falling apart.

Pour the olive oil then the lemon juice over the sarmas. Invert a second plate over them and press down gently. Pour in ⅔ cup (158 ml) water.

Set the pot over medium-high heat and bring the water to a boil. Reduce the heat, cover and simmer the sarmas for 1 hour. Halfway through the cooking process, check to see if additional water is needed. The pot should not dry out.

Let the sarmas cool for 15 minutes before carefully removing them from the pot to a serving plate.

feta cheese warmed in olive oil with raki

SERVES 4 TO 6

½ pound (227 g) Greek feta cheese

¼ cup (60 ml) olive oil

2 tablespoons Turkish rakı

1 teaspoon dried oregano

Juice of ½ lemon

1 teaspoon Aleppo pepper
(optional)

Sliced feta cheese and tumblers of rakı are a classic Anatolian combination. Here, we pair the two in the pan. When the rakı's alcohol burns off, a gentle hint of anise remains, melting into the creamy feta. Substitute ouzo or Pernod, if you wish. Serve with Grilled Flatbread (page 58) or pide chips.

Slice the feta cheese into equal pieces not more than 1-inch (25-mm) thick.

In a small cast-iron skillet over medium-low heat, warm the olive oil until it ripples. Lay the feta slices in a single layer in the oil.

Increase the heat to medium-high and fry the cheese for 1 minute. Add the rakı and oregano and fry for an additional 3 to 4 minutes until some of the alcohol burns off, the cheese becomes soft in the middle and the edges ooze into the olive oil. Do not turn the cheese. It may brown slightly at the edges, giving it a nice crust.

Remove the pan from the heat. Squeeze the lemon juice over the cheese. Dust with the Aleppo pepper, if using. Serve warm from the pan or slide the cheese and any browned bits clinging to the pan onto a warmed plate with curved sides.

CHAPTER 2

köfte and *kebabs*

THE CLEVER MOTHER MAKES SMALL MEATBALLS;
THE CLEVER CHILDREN GRAB TWO.
—*TURKISH PROVERB*

a skewer in time

Ground lamb köfte, fragrant with spices, are grilled on skewers.

On their adventures along the Aegean shores of Turkey in Homer's epic poem *Odyssey*, Odysseus and his crew partake of tenderized morsels of meat grilled on sticks—in other words, shish kebab (or *şiş kebap*). In Turkish, the word *şiş* means skewer and *kebap* means meat, although here in the States, *kebab* is used to refer to any type of food that's skewered and grilled.

You'll find kebab stands everywhere in Turkey, selling fragrant meat, usually lamb or chicken, wrapped in fresh, soft pide bread and dripping with garlicky yogurt çaçik sauce. This was the aroma that first struck us when we got off a bus in the seaside town of Göcek and walked along the narrow promenade. This region east of the Aegean toward the ruins of Aphrodisias is known for its roadside stands selling grilled kebabs. No matter that we had just eaten lunch—it was essential that we stop for a taste.

It would be unfair to call the equally popular köfte simply meatballs. Each Turkish home cook has a treasured family recipe in which minced lamb, beef or chicken is seasoned with a closely guarded mixture of cumin, pepper, allspice, even cinnamon, and shaped onto skewers for the grill. Many *locantas* (small restaurants) in Turkey serve köfte with mildly spicy grilled peppers and a refreshing glass of the yogurt drink Ayran (page 247), which not only adds a creamy-tart balance to the meat, but also is believed to aid in digestion.

Should you find yourself in a Turkish market, it's worth seeking out flat metal skewers capped with brass tips, often with pretty Ottoman designs such as the *lale*, or tulip, or the *tuğrâ*, the elegant calligraphic symbol of the sultans.

cLassic Lamb köfte

1½ pounds (781 g) ground lamb or beef

1 large egg, beaten

¼ cup (35 g) finely chopped shallots

1 teaspoon kosher salt

1 teaspoon Aleppo pepper

1 teaspoon ground cumin

½ teaspoon sweet paprika

½ teaspoon freshly ground black
    pepper

¼ cup (9 g) finely chopped parsley

¼ cup (13 g) finely chopped mint

4 to 6 metal or bamboo skewers
    (If using bamboo skewers, soak
    in water for 30 minutes before
    using.)

Vegetable oil, for brushing the grill

Perhaps the most popular dish in every Turkish locanta, the oval meatballs known as köfte are flavored with cumin, shallot and mint. They are an easy crowd pleaser that only taste better when the meat is mixed with seasonings at least 30 minutes before grilling. Here we use lamb, but beef is an option.

Serve the köfte on their own with Bulgur Pilaf with Fresh Herbs (page 128) or stuffed into Classic Puffed Pide Bread pockets (page 62) and always with plenty of Yogurt Dip with Cucumber and Mint (page 22). Grilled lamb köfte also pair well with Marinated Eggplant and Red Pepper Kebabs (page 43); you can alternate the köfte on the skewers with the eggplant cubes and onions and red bell peppers cut into 1½-inch (38-mm) pieces.

Line a baking sheet with foil. In a large bowl, combine the lamb, egg, shallots, salt, Aleppo pepper, cumin, paprika, black pepper, parsley and mint. Mix with your hands until well blended.

Shape 2 teaspoons of the meat mixture into an oval and flatten it slightly. Continue with the rest of the meat mixture, placing the köfte on the baking sheet in a single layer. Cover and refrigerate the tray of köfte for at least 30 minutes.

Heat a gas or charcoal grill to high. Thread the köfte onto the skewers. Most skewers will fit 4 to 5 köfte. We like to flatten them out slightly while molding the meat mixture around the skewer. Brush the grill with oil and place the köfte over direct heat for about 7 minutes, then turn and grill for 5 minutes more or until the centers reach 145°F (63°C). Serve hot.

VARIATION

To bake the köfte, heat the oven to 350°F (175°C). Prepare the meat mixture and chill for 30 minutes as directed above, but instead of threading onto the skewers, place

ALL IN THE FAMILY

When the soup is ready, Ipek sets the pot on a trivet in the center of her formal dining table, where eight family members have gathered. She ladles soup into bowls and drizzles the pepper-and-oil mixture over the top in whimsical shapes.

A feast lines up in dishes and pots across the table: roasted lamb shanks rubbed with mint and glistening with melted fat; *çig köfte*, raw lamb kneaded with bulgur, red pepper and lemon, shaped and placed on lettuce leaves; a shepherd salad of finely chopped hot green peppers, tomatoes, cucumbers and spring onions, dressed lightly with lemon and oil; and potatoes crisped in olive oil and spiced with cumin.

We applaud the cooks, who try to make us believe that the meal never would have been so delicious without our help. Sisters, cousins and aunties clear the table, shooing us onto a low divan in the living room with glasses of rakı.

The doorbell rings and another aunt arrives with two cousins.

"Now," says Ipek, looking at us with glee as she begins undulating her hips and moving her shoulders, "we must dance."

Nourishing and familiar, beans are part of the meal eaten to break the Ramadan fast.

on a baking sheet lined with parchment. Bake for 30 to 40 minutes, until the centers reach 145°F (63°C).

turkey sage köfte

1 pound (454 g) ground turkey

1 large egg, beaten

1 teaspoon kosher salt

½ teaspoon freshly ground black pepper

1 teaspoon dried mint, or
   1 tablespoon finely chopped fresh mint

1 teaspoon dried sumac

1 teaspoon finely chopped sage

1 large clove garlic, finely chopped

¼ cup (25 g) breadcrumbs

after returning to the United States from one of our Turkish journeys and longing for a good köfte, we created a turkey (as in the bird) version for family members and friends who no longer eat red meat. Because ground turkey is soft, we bake rather than grill these so they keep their shape. We first made them just before the Thanksgiving holiday, so we added sage, as is traditional, to the spice mix and served them with Sweet Potato Yufka (page 67). A bowl of Yogurt Dressing (page 97) on the side is essential.

Heat the oven to 350°F (175°C). Line a baking sheet with foil or parchment.

In a large bowl, combine the turkey, egg, salt, pepper, mint, sumac, sage, garlic and breadcrumbs. Mix with your hands until well blended.

Shape 2 teaspoons of the meat mixture into an oval and flatten it slightly. Continue with the rest of the meat mixture, placing the köfte on the baking sheet in a single layer.

Bake the turkey köfte for 25 minutes, until juices begin to run clear and the meat is cooked through but not dry.

WE BE COOKED MEAT ON TILE

—Sign at an outdoor restaurant in Cappadocia

marinated eggplant and red pepper kebabs

SERVES 4 TO 6

Pomegranate molasses mixed with olive oil, lemon and allspice makes a great marinade for meaty eggplant, which contrasts deliciously with bright squares of red bell pepper. These versatile kebabs go well with chicken or lamb chops or, when served atop a bed of pilaf, are a fine vegetarian main course. If grilling is not convenient, they can be cooked in a stovetop grill pan or in the oven.

½ cup (120 ml) olive oil
1 tablespoon pomegranate
    molasses
2 tablespoons lemon juice
1 tablespoon kosher salt
1 teaspoon ground allspice
½ teaspoon smoked paprika
1 large clove garlic, finely chopped

4 Japanese or 2 Italian eggplants
    (about 1½ pounds / 781 g),
    unpeeled
2 red bell peppers, cored and
    seeded
1 large sweet onion, peeled
Freshly ground black pepper to taste

4 to 6 metal or bamboo skewers
    (If using bamboo skewers, soak
    in water for 30 minutes before
    using.)
Vegetable oil, for brushing the grill

In a medium bowl, whisk together the olive oil, pomegranate molasses, lemon juice, salt, allspice, smoked paprika and garlic.

Cut each eggplant into pieces about 1½ inches (38 mm) square. Put in a bowl or shallow pan and add the marinade. Cover and refrigerate for at least 1 hour or up to 24 hours. If using the bell peppers and onions, do not add them to the marinade with the eggplant.

Heat a gas or charcoal grill to medium. Brush the skewers lightly with vegetable oil. Thread the eggplant sections on the skewers, alternating with bell peppers and onions and leaving a small space between the pieces so they cook evenly. Brush any remaining marinade over the vegetables.

Brush the grill lightly with vegetable oil and place the kebabs directly on the grate. Grill for 7 minutes, then turn and grill for 7 minutes more. The kebabs are ready when the eggplant is tender. They may also be cooked on the stovetop in a heavy grill pan, or baked in a 350°F (175°C) oven for 20 to 25 minutes.

Arrange the vegetable skewers on a platter. Season with a grind of black pepper before serving.

43

chickpea patties

2 tablespoons butter

½ cup (65 g) finely chopped onions
    or ½ cup (70 g) finely chopped
    shallots

4 cups minus 2 tablespoons
    (850 g) cooked chickpeas,
    or 2 (15-ounce / 425-g) cans
    chickpeas, drained

2 teaspoons Aleppo pepper

½ teaspoon kosher salt

1 teaspoon ground allspice

½ teaspoon ground cumin

½ teaspoon dried oregano

¼ cup (60 ml) vegetable stock or
    water

¼ cup (30 g) all-purpose flour

1 teaspoon baking powder

½ cup (120 ml) to 1 cup (236 ml)
    vegetable oil

Kalkan Ketchup (page 46), for
    serving)

Lemon wedges, for serving

akin to falafel, these golden vegetarian cakes, with their crisp coating and complex blend of spices, are deeply satisfying. We add a teaspoon of baking powder to keep the texture light, and serve them with the smooth beet condiment we call Kalkan Ketchup (page 46) for a sophisticated meat-less take on that guilty pleasure, chicken nuggets. Sometimes we change it up with Yogurt Dressing (page 97) and Grilled Flatbread (page 58).

In a saucepan over medium heat, melt the butter. Add the onions and cook until soft but not browned, about 5 minutes. Remove from the heat and cool slightly.

Put the chickpeas, Aleppo pepper, salt, allspice, cumin and oregano in a food processor and pulse to just blend or mash by hand with a fork.

Add the onions, butter and vegetable stock to the processor and pulse again until just combined. The mixture should remain coarse; do not pulse to a completely smooth puree.

In a bowl, sift together the flour and baking powder and add to the chick-peas. Pulse until thoroughly incorporated. Transfer the mixture to the bowl, cover and refrigerate for 30 minutes or up to 24 hours.

Shape 1 heaping tablespoon of the chickpea mixture into a round, evenly flattened, 2-inch (5-cm) patty. Place on a lightly oiled baking sheet or dish large enough to hold them in a single layer. Continue with the rest of the chickpea mixture.

Pour ¼ inch (6 mm) of the vegetable oil into a wide, heavy pan over medi-um-high heat. Heat the oil until it sizzles when a drop of water hits it.

Carefully add the patties to the oil in batches (do not crowd the pan) and fry 2 to 3 minutes per side until deep golden brown. Transfer to a paper towel–lined tray and keep warm in a low oven until all have been fried. Serve with Kalkan Ketchup on the side and lemon wedges.

kalkan ketchup

MAKES 3 CUPS (709 ml)

1 pound (454 grams) red beets, or a mix of red and golden beets

1 cup (236 ml) distilled white vinegar

½ cup packed (110 g) light brown sugar

⅓ cup (45 g) chopped shallots

1 teaspoon kosher salt

½ teaspoon ground cumin

½ teaspoon ground coriander

½ teaspoon freshly ground black pepper

With a nod to the Mediterranean resort town where we enjoyed many dishes made with beets, this versatile condiment makes a splendid accompaniment to Chickpea Patties (page 44) and many other vegetarian köfte. It also goes well with burgers, meat köfte and Aegean Oven-Fried Potatoes (page 204), and serves as a savory spread with goat cheese and crackers on the meze table. The beets may be roasted one day in advance.

Heat the oven to 400°F (204°C). Line a baking sheet with enough overhanging foil to cover the beets.

Halve the beets and lay them cut side down on the baking sheet. Cover with the overhanging foil and bake for 45 minutes, or until tender.

When cool enough to handle, peel and dice the beets and put in a medium saucepan. Add the vinegar, light brown sugar, shallots, salt, cumin, coriander and pepper. Over high heat, bring the mixture to a boil. Reduce the heat to low and simmer for 20 minutes.

Spoon the mixture into a food processor or blender and pulse until it becomes a smooth puree. Taste and add more salt, if needed. Kalkan Ketchup will keep for 3 weeks in a sealed jar in the refrigerator.

chicken shish kebabs

SERVES 4 TO 6

the marinade for these kebabs was inspired by a Persian friend who now lives in the fashionable Cihangir District on Istanbul's European side. She adapted her mother's recipe for grilled chicken by incorporating Turkish spices into the yogurt marinade, with lemony sumac and sweet paprika for brightness and color, and smoked paprika for depth.

These kebabs are great fun to serve at a backyard party. They may be cooked on the grill or baked in the oven. We always make extra because kebabs taste even better the next day as a savory addition to a main dish salad. In addition to making the chicken meltingly tender, the yogurt marinade ensures that the meat remains moist. Set out on platters accompanied by Classic Puffed Pide Bread (page 62) or Sweet Potato Yufka (page 67), with serving bowls of Yogurt Dressing (page 97) and tart, juicy Shepherd's Salad (page 96).

---

1 ½ teaspoons ground sumac

1 ½ tablespoons dried mint

1 teaspoon smoked paprika

1 teaspoon sweet paprika

1 ½ teaspoons kosher salt

1 teaspoon freshly ground black pepper

1 tablespoon lemon juice

2 cups (480 ml) plain yogurt

2 cloves garlic, minced

½ cup (55 g) chopped onion

2 tablespoons olive oil

1 medium sweet onion

1½ pounds (781 g) boneless, skinless chicken breasts or thighs, or a combination, cut into 1½-inch (38 mm) pieces

6 to 8 metal or bamboo skewers (If using bamboo skewers, soak in water for 30 minutes before using.)

Vegetable oil, for brushing the grill

In a bowl large enough to accommodate all the chicken pieces, combine the sumac, mint, smoked paprika, sweet paprika, salt, pepper and lemon juice. Add the yogurt, garlic, chopped onions and olive oil and mix well.

Add the chicken pieces to the yogurt-spice mixture and stir to completely cover the meat with the marinade. Cover the bowl with plastic wrap or foil and marinate the chicken in the refrigerator for at least 1 hour and up to 24 hours.

Heat a gas or charcoal grill to medium-high. Peel the sweet onion and cut it into 1½- (38- to 50-mm) pieces. Separate the onion layers.

Alternate threading 4 to 6 chicken pieces with larger onion pieces on each skewer. Leave space between the pieces of chicken so that they cook evenly.

Lightly brush the grill with vegetable oil and place the skewers on the hot grill. Close the lid and cook for 6 minutes, then turn the skewers over and cook

(RECIPE CONTINUES)

Cooks prepare for a busy night on Istiklal Avenue in Beyoglu, Istanbul.

for 5 to 6 minutes on the second side until the juices begin to run clear and the internal temperature reaches 165°F (74°C) to 170°F (77°C). Arrange the skewers on a platter.

Lamb shish kebab with pomegranate and soy sauce

SERVES 6

althoum lamb is most authentically Turkish, we find this marinade also works well with beef sirloin tips. In Turkey, only onions are skewered with the meat; other vegetables are always grilled separately. The tangy pomegranate-soy sauce marinade ensures a delectable crust on the grilled meat. Stuff the delicious kebab into Classic Puffed Pide Bread (page 62) and drizzle with Yogurt Dressing (page 97).

In a bowl large enough to hold the meat, whisk together the sunflower oil, pomegranate molasses, soy sauce, salt, cumin, paprika and garlic.

Add the meat to the marinade and ensure it is completely submerged. Cover and marinate in the refrigerator for at least 1 hour and up to 3 hours.

Core and seed the pepper and cut it into 1½-inch (38-mm) pieces. Prick the cherry tomatoes with a toothpick to prevent them from bursting on the grill.

Brush 6 of the skewers with vegetable oil. Alternate threading the tomatoes and pepper pieces onto the skewers, dividing evenly among the skewers. Brush the vegetables with vegetable oil and season with salt.

Heat a gas or charcoal grill to medium-high. Place the vegetable skewers directly on the grate and grill the vegetables for 10 to 15 minutes, turning to brown all sides and brushing occasionally with more vegetable oil.

When the vegetables are tender, arrange the skewers on a serving platter. Keep warm while grilling the meat.

Brush the remaining skewers with vegetable oil. Peel the onion and cut it into 1½-inch to 2-inch (38-mm to 51-mm) pieces. Alternately thread pieces of lamb with onion segments on each skewer. Leave a bit of space between the meat so that it cooks evenly.

Place the skewers on the hot grill and close the lid. Cook for 6 minutes.

(RECIPE CONTINUES)

½ cup (120 ml) sunflower or
    grapeseed oil

3 tablespoons pomegranate
    molasses

2 tablespoons soy sauce

1 teaspoon kosher salt

1 teaspoon ground cumin

½ teaspoon sweet paprika

1 large clove garlic, finely chopped

1½ pounds (781 g) leg of lamb or
    beef sirloin, cut into 1½-inch
    (38-mm) pieces

1 bell pepper, any color

12 to 18 cherry tomatoes

¼ cup (60 ml) vegetable oil for
    brushing the vegetables

Kosher salt

1 medium sweet onion

12 metal or bamboo skewers
(If using bamboo skewers, soak
    in water for 30 minutes before
    using.)

Vegetable oil, for brushing the grill

Turn the skewers over and cook for an additional 6 minutes or until the internal temperature reaches 140°F (60°C).

You can remove the meat and vegetables from the skewers and serve them separately on platters if you wish, or simply leave them on their skewers.

KEEP CALM AND HAVE A KEBAB
—Sign in the window of a New
York City kebab shop

flatbreads, börek and more

THE BREAD'S BEAUTY IS BORN BY THE YEAST'S SWELLING.

—TURKISH PROVERB

the Drama of the Dough

Shaping gözleme in a café on the Divan Yolu, Istanbul.

Of the many reasons we keep returning to Turkey, the abundant and delectable varieties of freshly baked bread are a pleasure that keeps drawing us back. Hot, crusty loaves pulled from a wood-fired oven are a welcome companion to every meal.

We've savored Turkish breads in southeastern cities from Urfa to Dyarbakir to Mardin, in homes with four concrete walls, a dirt floor and an outdoor oven, as well as in modern apartments with the latest stoves. We've enjoyed *yufka*, made with wheat flour, water and table salt, baked on a flat griddle and folded around lamb kebabs or cheese, herbs and vegetables from the backyard garden. Yufka's versatility is nearly endless. When the sheets are stretched paper-thin, layered with butter or oil and savory or sweet fillings, yufka becomes börek and baklava: two crisp, layered, irresistible pastries.

Oversized loaves of sourdough bread, appear throughout Turkey, sliced and served at breakfast with cheese, olives and honey, and at lunch beside a filling soup bowl of *çorba*. Bread appears as a meze in the form of *gözleme*, which is yufka stuffed with cheese and herbs and grilled to toasty perfection.

But the bread that won our hearts after that first visit to Istanbul and remains our favorite is the honey-gold, sesame-studded, crisp and chewy ring called *simit*, Turkey's quintessential street food. Comparable to a bagel or the German soft pretzel, it's an inexpensive and delicious snack. The sesame seed crust has a slight sweetness, and the chewy interior is fragrant and moreish. Anyone who has visited Istanbul in the last five hundred years will be familiar with the simit seller balancing a tray of bread rings on his head, or with the modern glass-enclosed carts where, when a fresh batch arrives, the seller calls, *"Taze, yeni geldi, Çıtır!"* (Fresh, newly arrived, crispy!)

stuffed flatbread (gözleme)

SERVES 4 TO 6

1 to 2 teaspoons olive oil

1 recipe Flatbread Dough (recipe
follows)

8 ounces (153 g) crumbled feta
cheese

1 cup (50 g) chopped flat-leaf
parsley

We first tasted gözleme, our favorite Turkish fast food, at an outdoor kiosk on a bus route near the ancient city of Ephesus. On that sunlit afternoon, the friendly cook, wearing pink-and-yellow-flowered shalwar trousers and a pink headscarf, rolled dough over a wooden board with a thin dowel, then placed it on a hot stone, sprinkling it with feta and parsley. When the edges began to crisp and the underside was dotted with bubbles, she folded the dough, flipped it and grilled it until the cheese softened. Reminiscent of both a Mexican quesadilla and a French handheld crepe, gözleme is served everywhere. Tender, fragrant and piquant with feta, it's easy to make at home in a frying pan or on the grill.

Heat a large cast-iron skillet or griddle over high heat until it is very hot. Lightly brush the cooking surface with olive oil.

Place one flatbread in the skillet (or as many as will fit on the griddle) and sprinkle one half of the dough round with feta and parsley. Fold to enclose the filling. Cook, flipping once, until both sides are lightly browned, about 2 minutes on each side. Remove to a platter and keep warm until all of the gözleme have been made. Slice each flatbread into 6 pieces and serve immediately.

fLatBReaD DOUGh

These flatbreads are cooked in a frying pan, more like a tortilla than a pita bread with a pocket. Yogurt adds pleasant flavor and helps create a tender, pliable dough that is easy to roll out and shape.

2½ cups (315 g) all-purpose flour
1 teaspoon kosher salt
1 cup (240 ml) plain yogurt
1 tablespoon vegetable oil

Sift the flour and salt into the bowl of a stand mixer fitted with a dough hook. Add the yogurt and mix for 7 to 10 minutes to form a smooth, pliable dough. If the dough is too sticky, dust with a little more flour; if it's too dry, add up to 3 tablespoons water, 1 tablespoon at a time.

Coat the inside of a large bowl with the vegetable oil. Form the dough into a ball and place it in the bowl. Cover with a clean, damp kitchen towel and let it rest in a warm place for about 30 minutes.

Turn the dough out onto a lightly floured surface and divide into 6 equal pieces. Form each piece into a ball then roll each ball into a thin, almost translucent 6-inch (15-cm) round. Keep the remaining dough covered while rolling out each piece. Stack the rounds of dough between waxed paper or parchment so they don't stick together. At this point, you can wrap the stacked rounds in plastic and refrigerate for up to 24 hours, or freeze for up to 1 month. Bring to room temperature before using. Otherwise, proceed to either Grilled Flatbread (page 58) or Stuffed Flatbread (page 56).

grilled flatbread (yufka)

making flatbread to eat with meze or dinner is about as easy at it gets. Here we put the rounds of dough on the grill, flipping once or twice until the edges crisp. Serve stacked on a plate to wrap around fillings or torn into pieces to dip into hummus. The flatbread will keep well for a day or two wrapped in plastic. The traditional way to revive flatbread that's becomes brittle is to brush each side with water and let it rest under a tea towel for a minute or two, then briefly reheat it in a skillet or on the grill, flipping once, to soften.

1 to 2 teaspoons olive oil

1 recipe Flatbread Dough (page 57), formed into rounds

Flaky sea salt (optional)

Heat a large cast-iron skillet until it is very hot, or heat a griddle or grill to high. Lightly brush the cooking surface with olive oil.

Place 1 round of rolled-out dough in the skillet (or as many as will fit on the griddle or grill) and cook until the bottom is lightly browned, about 2 minutes. Keep the remaining rounds of dough covered with a clean, damp kitchen towel until ready to use.

Flip the dough to brown the other side, 1½ to 2 minutes. The bread may puff up while cooking, but it will deflate when cooled. When both sides are brown, slide the flatbread onto a platter and, while still warm, sprinkle with flaky sea salt if desired. Serve the flatbread warm or at room temperature.

Dervishes practicing moving meditation in the garden of the Mevlana Museum in Konya

TO SEE A DERVISH

As we hike up a ridge leading into the mountains toward the town of Elmali, we pass a tree tied with rags and wisps of cloth holding prayers and wishes. The sacred tree marks the way to a tomb outside the village that holds the bones of a dervish named Abdal Musa.

A few weeks earlier, we had taken the local bus through lush countryside filled with apple orchards to Musa's resting place in a grove of pines. An old man in a blue knit cap, with one of the most peaceful faces we have ever seen, stood at the entrance to the tomb. He pressed his hand to his heart and said, "I am a dervish too."

Enveloped in the scent of pine, we watched pilgrims pray before Musa's tomb, which was draped in a green cloth. For the first time in weeks, we felt at peace and protected, as if Musa's spirit wished for all to be well.

TURKISH PIZZA (LAHMACUN)

FOR THE DOUGH

1 teaspoon active dry yeast

½ teaspoon sugar

1 cup (236 ml) lukewarm water, divided

3 cups (375 g) all-purpose flour

½ teaspoon kosher salt

½ teaspoon vegetable oil

FOR THE TOPPING

1 tablespoon butter

2 tablespoons olive oil, divided

1 medium onion, finely chopped

2 cloves garlic, finely chopped

¾ teaspoon kosher salt, divided

½ pound (227 g) ground lamb

2 tablespoons tomato paste

1 teaspoon Aleppo pepper

1½ teaspoons dried oregano

1½ teaspoons dried mint

1½ teaspoons ground sumac

½ teaspoon freshly ground black pepper

FOR SERVING

1 to 2 lemons, cut into wedges

½ cup (18 g) coarsely chopped parsley

1 large tomato, sliced

SERVES 4 TO 6

at lunchtime in Istanbul, merchants will send out for lahmacun and cups of *ayran*, the refreshing yogurt drink (page 247). This savory meat-topped flatbread has been a staple in Turkey, Armenia and Syria since at least the second century BCE; to this day it remains a popular fast food throughout Turkey, and there are lahmacun ovens to be found in almost every neighborhood.

This is a fun recipe to make with friends. Along with classic lamb topping, we set out chopped tomatoes, olives, chopped onions, chopped preserved lemon, finely shredded string cheese and a handful of herbs from the garden, then let guests roll out the dough and experiment. Feel free to substitute ground beef or turkey for the lamb. The key to perfect lahmucun is to make sure the ingredients are all finely chopped or shredded, and to use a light touch when layering them over the crust.

Make the dough: In a small bowl, mix the yeast, sugar and ⅓ cup (79 ml) lukewarm water. Set aside until it starts to foam, about 15 minutes.

In the bowl of a stand mixer fitted with the dough hook, sift together the flour and salt. (If making the dough by hand, mix in a medium bowl and make a well in the center.)

Pour the yeast mixture into the flour and add the remaining ⅔ cup (158 ml) warm water. Set mixer to medium speed and incorporate the liquid into the flour until most of the liquid is absorbed and a somewhat shaggy dough is formed. Add a bit of extra water if the dough seems too dry, or a small amount of extra flour if it is too sticky.

Continue to knead the dough for 7 to 10 minutes until it becomes elastic and smooth. If kneading by hand, turn the dough onto a floured board and make one-quarter turns at regular intervals.

Coat a large bowl with vegetable oil and place the dough in the bowl. Cover with a damp kitchen towel and leave in a warm place for 1 hour or until the dough doubles in size.

Heat the oven to 425°F (218°C). If using a pizza stone, heat the stone starting in a cold oven, or line a baking sheet with parchment and set aside.

Make the topping: Melt the butter and 1 tablespoon olive oil in a medium skillet over moderate heat. Add the onions, garlic and ¼ teaspoon salt. Sauté until the onions are soft and translucent but not brown, about 6 to 8 minutes.

In a medium bowl, combine the lamb, tomato paste, Aleppo pepper, oregano, mint, sumac, the remaining ½ teaspoon salt and black pepper. Add the sautéed onions and garlic.

When the dough has doubled in size, turn it out onto a lightly floured surface. Cut the dough into quarters. With floured fingers, shape the dough into four ¼-inch (6-mm) thick round or oblong pizzas. If necessary, use a rolling pin to flatten each piece.

Place one flatbread on the parchment-lined baking sheet or on a pizza peel, lightly coated with flour. Brush the edges of the dough with some of the remaining olive oil to create a crisp crust. Spread a thin layer of the topping mixture evenly over the dough. Place the baking sheet into the oven or slide the flatbread from the peel onto the pizza. Bake for about 15 minutes until the edges begin to turn golden and the lamb topping is browned.

Remove the lahmacun from the oven and slide it onto a cutting board. Cut into 4 to 6 wedges. Repeat with the remaining dough and toppings to make three more pizzas. Serve immediately with lemon wedges, parsley and fresh tomato slices.

cLassic puffed pide bread

2 teaspoons active dry yeast

½ teaspoon sugar

½ cup (120 ml) lukewarm water

2 cups (250 g) all-purpose flour

½ teaspoon kosher salt

1 tablespoon olive oil

1 tablespoon plain yogurt

½ teaspoon vegetable oil

1 large egg, beaten

Flaky sea salt

Sesame seeds (optional)

Nigella seeds (optional)

What's in a name? The ancient Greeks of Anatolia brought the word *pita* or *pide* into the Turkish lexicon. It means bread in Aramaic, a language related to Hebrew that is still spoken in Christian neighborhoods in southeastern Turkey and in Syrian Orthodox churches throughout the world. But do not confuse Turkish pide with the familiar Middle Eastern pocket bread. It's confusing enough, because in Turkey pide is actually used to describe three different types of bread: a flatbread similar to pita, a boat-shaped dough that is filled before baking (page 64) and this pide, a puffed bread topped with sesame and nigella seeds.

This flatbread pide relies on yeast to give it lift and a soft bread-like interior. Slice and fill it with kebabs or leftover roast chicken, lettuce and tomato. We tear pide into bite-sized pieces to scoop into Baked Hummus with Pine Nuts (page 23), Carrot Hummus with Toasted Fennel Seeds (page 24), Kalkan Ketchup (page 46) and Yogurt Dip with Cucumber and Mint (page 22).

In a small bowl combine the yeast, sugar and water. Let the mixture sit until it foams, about 15 minutes.

In the bowl of a stand mixer fitted with a dough hook, combine the flour and salt. (Or mix by hand in a medium bowl and make a well in the center.)

Add the yeast mixture, olive oil and yogurt to the flour. Slowly incorporate the wet ingredients into the dry ingredients on low speed, adding a tablespoon of water at a time, if needed, until a sticky dough is formed. Knead the dough on low speed in the mixer for 5 to 7 minutes, until it becomes pliable and silky and pulls away from the sides of the bowl, or knead it by hand on a lightly floured surface.

Coat a large bowl with vegetable oil, turn the dough into the bowl and cover with a damp kitchen towel. Let the dough rise in a warm, draft-free place until it doubles in size, about 1 hour. (Or leave to rise in the refrigerator overnight.)

Heat the oven to 425°F (218°C). If using a pizza stone, heat the stone starting in a cold oven, or lightly oil a baking sheet and set aside.

To form the pide, sprinkle flour on a clean work surface. Turn the dough out and fold it onto itself 3 or 4 times to deflate. Cut into 4 equal pieces.

Shape each pide into a 6- to 7-inch (150- to 175-mm) round. Brush the tops with the beaten egg. Leave the tops plain or sprinkle them with salt, sesame or nigella seeds, or a combination of all three.

Place the pide directly on the heated pizza stone or oiled baking sheet and bake until puffy and golden brown on top, about 15 minutes. Remove from the oven, slide onto a tray or plate and serve.

cheese-filled bread boat (peinirli)

2 teaspoons active dry yeast

½ teaspoon sugar

½ to ⅔ cup (120 to 158 ml) lukewarm water

2 cups (250 g) all-purpose flour

½ teaspoon kosher salt

1 tablespoon olive oil

1 tablespoon plain yogurt

½ teaspoon vegetable oil

4 ounces (110 g) crumbled feta cheese (see page 66)

⅓ cup (12 g) roughly chopped parsley

1 large egg, beaten

Our travels in the Turkish countryside always remind us of the generosity of the people. While driving through the southwestern Aegean region one spring morning, we spotted a group of women baking bread in an outdoor communal oven. We pulled over and got out of the car to take a few photographs. Minutes later, after much laughter and warm hugs, we left with a loaf of fragrant hot flatbread in the shape of a boat, stuffed with creamy feta and fresh chopped parsley. This bread, also called pide (page 62), is commonly stuffed with a ground meat mixture as well. Serve with Dill-Stuffed Whole Fish Baked in Salt (page 167) and Shepherd's Salad (page 96).

In a small bowl combine the yeast, sugar and ½ cup (120 ml) lukewarm water. Let the mixture sit until it foams, about 15 minutes.

In the bowl of a stand mixer fitted with a dough hook, mix the flour and salt. (Or mix by hand in a medium bowl and make a well in the center.)

Add the yeast mixture, olive oil and yogurt to the flour. Slowly incorporate the wet ingredients into the dry ingredients on low speed, adding more water, a tablespoonful at a time, if needed, until a sticky dough is formed. Knead the dough on low speed in the mixer for 5 to 7 minutes, until it becomes pliable and pulls away from the sides of the bowl, or knead it by hand on a floured surface.

Coat the inside of a large bowl with vegetable oil, turn the dough into the bowl and cover the bowl with plastic wrap or a damp kitchen towel. Let the dough rise in a warm, draft-free place until the dough doubles in size, about 1 hour. (It also may be left to rise overnight in the refrigerator.)

Heat the oven to 425°F (218°C). If using a pizza stone, heat the stone starting in a cold oven, or line a baking sheet with parchment and set aside.

To form the bread boat, dust a clean work surface with flour. Turn the dough

(RECIPE CONTINUES)

out on the board and fold it onto itself 3 or 4 times to deflate. Roll out into a rectangle about 6 inches (15 cm) wide, 12 to 14 inches (30 to 36 cm) long and ¾ inch (19 mm) thick.

Sprinkle the dough with the feta cheese and parsley, leaving 1½ inches (38 mm) on each edge. Roll the long sides of the dough over the filling, leaving about 3 inches (75 mm) of the cheese and parsley mixture exposed. Pinch the top and bottom of the dough to form the bow and stern of the boat. Brush the edges with the beaten egg and carefully transfer to the pizza stone or baking sheet.

Bake for 15 to 20 minutes, until the crust is puffy and browned, and the cheese has melted on top.

Note: The feta and parsley filling can be replaced with 1 medium tomato, thinly sliced and layered evenly over the dough, topped with 4 ounces (110 g) crumbled goat cheese and 1 to 2 tablespoons crumbled Crisp Roasted Olives (optional, page 108).

sweet potato yufka

MAKES 6 FLATBREADS

We met Sakir outside his antique shop in Kalkan, a town nestled into the foothills of the Taurus Mountains overlooking the turquoise Mediterranean. His shop may have been filled with Ottoman treasures, but we bonded over a shared passion for food. Sakir taught us to cook many Turkish dishes, including a simple, perfect shish kebab and his mother's beet salad (page 207), in the process becoming a dear friend who has since cooked in our own kitchens. His brilliantly simple sweet potato flatbread cooks up as fast as pancakes and disappears quickly. Serve with Turkey Sage Köfte (page 42) and Chicken Shish Kebabs (page 47).

2 medium sweet potatoes, baked, peeled and mashed, or 1 (15-ounce / 425-g) can sweet potato puree

2 cups (250 g) all-purpose flour

1 teaspoon kosher salt

2 tablespoons olive oil

In a food processor fitted with a metal blade, combine the mashed sweet potatoes, flour, salt and olive oil. Pulse to combine. Once the mixture holds together, process the dough on low for 3 to 5 minutes, or until the dough becomes pliable. If the dough is too sticky, add more flour, 1 tablespoon at a time.

Turn the dough out onto a lightly floured surface and knead it for about 1 minute. Shape the dough into a ball and let it rest for 30 minutes.

Heat a griddle or large skillet over high heat. Divide the dough into 6 balls. Roll each ball into a round about ¼-inch (6-mm) thick. Place 1 or 2 flatbreads on the griddle and cook for 2 to 3 minutes, until the bottom begins to brown and the kitchen fills with the aroma of sweet potatoes.

Flip the flatbread and cook it another 2 to 3 minutes until the underside is brown and the flatbread is crisp. Repeat with the remaining dough. Serve warm.

CRISPY BÖREK WITH FETA, PARSLEY AND PRESERVED LEMON

MAKES 24 (2-INCH / 5-CM) SQUARES

2 cups (300 g) crumbled feta
  cheese

2 tablespoons plain yogurt

½ cup (40 g) finely chopped
  preserved lemons, rinsed, or
  2 tablespoons finely chopped
  lemon zest

½ cup (115 g / 1 stick) butter

½ pound (227 g) filo dough, thawed
  at room temperature

1 cup (35 g) roughly chopped
  parsley

½ teaspoon sweet paprika

In Greece, Turkey and the Middle East, böreks—flaky pastries filled with cheese or meat—appear in nearly every bus station food stand and restaurant, and on most home tables as well. Cheese börek is easy to make and wonderful to eat as a light main course with a green salad. Cut into smaller pieces, börek becomes a perfect starter or meze.

Börek also freezes well. To reheat, place the frozen pastries in a 350°F (175°C) oven for 20 to 25 minutes.

Heat the oven to 350°F (175°C). Put the crumbled feta in a bowl and add the yogurt and lemon. Mash to create a creamy but still coarse mixture.

In a small saucepan, melt the butter over low heat. Unroll the filo dough and place it on a clean work surface. Cover the filo with a damp kitchen towel to prevent it from drying out.

Brush a thin layer of melted butter in the bottom of a 13 by 8-inch (33 by 20-cm) baking pan. Carefully place 2 sheets of filo dough in the bottom of the pan. Lightly brush the butter over the surface of the dough. Coat the edges with butter to seal the layers. Continue layering the filo dough, coating each layer with the butter until you have used half of the sheets and half of the butter.

Spread the cheese mixture evenly over the dough and sprinkle the parsley over the cheese. Cover with a sheet of filo and continue layering the remaining dough over the filling, brushing each sheet with butter. When all the filo sheets are used, brush the entire surface of the börek with the remaining butter.

Use a sharp knife to cut the börek into 2-inch (5-cm) squares. Dust the top lightly with paprika.

Bake until golden brown and puffed, 30 to 35 minutes. If the börek begins to brown too quickly, cover with a sheet of parchment. Remove the parchment 1 minute before removing the börek from the oven.

 Yufka, the versatile flatbread dough, finds its way into many meals.

Cut the squares apart and serve warm or at room temperature as part of a meze table.

Börek may be made one day ahead and reheated in a 400°F (204°C) oven for 5 to 10 minutes.

Sunday Simits

1 teaspoon active dry yeast

1¼ cups (295 ml) warm water

3 cups (375 g) all-purpose flour, divided

¾ teaspoon kosher salt

½ teaspoon vegetable oil

1 cup (150 g) hulled, raw sesame seeds

¼ cup (60 ml) grape molasses or honey

½ cup (120 ml) lukewarm water, divided

Flaky sea salt (optional)

1 cup (236 ml) boiling water

Simits are Istanbul's iconic street food, piled on dowels and eaten out of hand like a soft pretzel. With a hint of sweetness from grape molasses, the doughnut-shaped bread's crisp exterior yields to a flavorful, slightly chewy center. Intriguingly crusted in sesame seeds, simits are often served at breakfast with butter and honey or soft cheese and local fruit preserves. At home, we invite friends for Simits Sundays, when we treat the simits like bagels in a cultural brunch mash-up, with smoked salmon, sliced feta, thin red onion rings, capers and lemon. Simits are also irresistible when eaten with just a little too much butter.

The dough should be prepared the night before you plan to bake it, as simits require a slow rise in the refrigerator. To achieve the proper texture, they are baked above a pan of boiling water placed in the bottom of the oven to create a steamy environment. Trust us—they are well worth these small bits of extra effort.

In the bowl of a stand mixer fitted with the dough hook, dissolve the dry yeast in the warm water. Let the yeast sit until it foams, about 15 minutes.

Add 1 cup (125 g) of the flour and the salt to the yeast mixture. With the mixer on low, gradually add enough of the remaining flour until a stiff dough forms. Knead for 10 to 12 minutes. You can also mix the initial cup of flour with the yeast mixture in a bowl by hand, dump the remaining flour onto a clean work surface, then incorporate the dough into the flour and knead it by hand.

Use the vegetable oil to coat a bowl large enough to allow the dough to double in size. Shape the dough into a ball, place it into the bowl and cover with plastic. Set in the refrigerator to rise for 8 to 10 hours. The dough may be left in the refrigerator for up to 24 hours.

(RECIPE CONTINUES)

There were a total of 300 sellers and 70 bakeries that made simits five times each day. The last batch came out after dark, and the sellers threaded the rings onto long sticks fixed into the corners of their baskets or trays, and hung a small lantern at the top to attract the attention of the crowds on their way home after work.

—*Evliya Çelebi, seventeenth-century Turkish historian*

When ready to bake, heat the oven to 450°F (232°C). Line a baking sheet with parchment.

Put the sesame seeds into a medium heavy skillet over moderate heat. Toss and stir until the seeds turn light golden, about 7 minutes. Don't walk away! If the seeds get dark, they will turn bitter. Transfer to a wide, shallow bowl and let cool.

Remove the dough from the refrigerator; it should now be doubled in size. Lightly dust a clean work surface with flour and turn the dough onto it. Punch down the dough until it deflates.

Divide the dough into 8 equal pieces, forming each into a ball. Keep the dough balls covered with a damp kitchen towel to prevent them from drying out.

Dust your hands with flour. Take a ball of dough and, working from the center out, begin rolling it between your palms to create a rope. Roll and stretch the dough until it is approximately 16 to 18 inches (10 to 46 cm) long.

With one hand holding the dough-rope in the center, lift it from the work surface. With the other hand, pinch the 2 ends together at the bottom. Twist the rope 4 or 5 times to create an interlocking spiral. Lay the dough on the work surface, and shape it into a ring about 4 inches (10 cm) in diameter. Squeeze the ends together.

Continue with the other balls of dough, keeping the rings covered until you have 8 rings, about 4 inches (10 cm) in diameter. Keep the dough rings covered with a damp towel. Let the rings rest for 30 minutes.

In a shallow bowl wide enough to hold a simit, combine the grape molasses with ¼ cup (60 ml) lukewarm water and stir to dissolve. Place the bowl with the molasses mixture on the counter. Next to it, place a cake rack over paper towels or newspaper to catch any drippings. Place the sesame seeds next to the cake rack and place the prepared baking sheet next to the bowl of seeds.

Gently lift each simit ring so that it holds its shape and dip the dough into the molasses mixture to coat the entire ring. Set the simit on the cake rack to

(RECIPE CONTINUES)

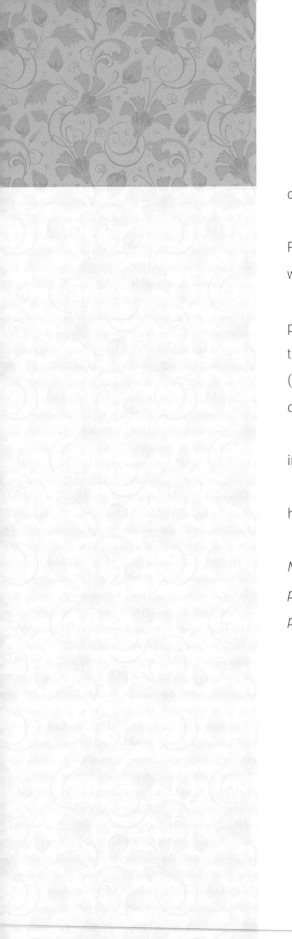

drain and repeat the process with the 7 remaining simits.

To finish, dip each ring into the sesame seeds and coat the entire simit. Place the simits on the baking sheet and carefully reshape as needed. Sprinkle with flaky sea salt, if desired.

Place an empty baking dish on the lowest rack in the oven and carefully pour 1 cup (236 ml) of boiling water into the dish. Place the baking sheet with the simits on the rack above the water. Carefully sprinkle the remaining ¼ cup (60 ml) of lukewarm water onto the floor of the oven and quickly close the oven door. The steam will create a crisp and chewy simit.

After 10 minutes, carefully remove the dish of hot water and continue baking simits for an additional 10 minutes or until they are a rich golden brown.

Simits can be frozen for up to 3 months and regain their crispness when heated in a 350°F (175°C) oven.

Note: Instead of sesame seeds, you can coat the simits with 1 cup (125 g) nigella or poppy seeds, or a mixture of all three. It is not necessary to toast the nigella or poppy seeds.

gougères a la turka

MAKES 32 GOUGÈRES

In the lakeshore suburb of Milwaukee, Wisconsin, where Joy grew up, women like her mother became newly sophisticated cooks under the influence of Julia Child. Timeworn cocktail party recipes were abandoned and suddenly these ethereal puffs called gougères were being served with gimlets and Manhattans. Airy yet rich, gougères seemed a miracle—and they still do. Given our interest in Anatolian culture, it was perhaps inevitable that we would end up making them with feta and Aleppo pepper. We tell ourselves they would have been praised by French-trained chefs in the sultan's court. They just beg to be served with champagne, and are also a sophisticated surprise on a meze platter.

Heat the oven to 375°F (190°C). Line a baking sheet with parchment or a Silpat.

Make the basic gougères dough: Melt the butter in a medium heavy saucepan over low heat. Turn heat to medium-high and add water. Stir until the butter melts and the mixture comes to a boil. Remove from the heat.

Quickly add the flour to the butter mixture all at once and stir vigorously until the dough pulls away from the sides of the pan and forms a ball. Allow the pan to cool slightly, about 5 minutes.

When the mixture is warm to the touch, but no longer hot, add the first egg, stirring in a figure-8 motion until the egg is completely incorporated. Add the remaining eggs one at a time, fully incorporating each before adding the next. The mixture will transform into a golden, glossy unctuous paste. (To make the dough in a food processor, see page 76.)

To make the feta gougères, add the cheese and stir gently to incorporate it into the paste.

Using a teaspoon, scoop a dollop of the paste about 1½ (38 mm) inches

(RECIPE CONTINUES)

FOR BASIC DOUGH

½ cup (115 g / 1 stick) butter

1 cup (236 ml) water

1 cup (125 g) all-purpose flour

4 large eggs at room temperature

FOR FETA GOUGÈRES

½ cup (75 g) finely crumbled feta cheese

1 teaspoon sweet paprika

1 teaspoon flaky sea salt

FOR NIGELLA GOUGÈRES

1 tablespoon nigella seeds

1 tablespoon flaky sea salt

FOR ALEPPO PEPPER GOUGÈRES

1 tablespoon Aleppo pepper

1 tablespoon flaky sea salt

in diameter and drop it onto the prepared baking sheet, using a second spoon to help release it. Repeat with the remaining dough, placing the gougères about 1 inch (25 mm) apart.

Dust the gougères with paprika and a sprinkling of flaky sea salt and bake for 25 to 30 minutes, until puffed and pale golden brown.

To make the nigella seed gougères, prepare the basic dough as described above, but do not add the feta cheese. Before baking, sprinkle with the nigella seeds and flaky sea salt.

To make the Aleppo pepper gougères, prepare the basic dough as described above, but do not add the feta cheese. Before baking, sprinkle with Aleppo pepper and flaky sea salt.

Baked gougères may be frozen for up to 2 months and reheated in a 350°F (175°C) oven for 10 to 15 minutes.

Note: To make the basic gougère dough in a food processor, melt the butter and combine it with the water and flour on the stovetop, then transfer the mixture to the work bowl of a food processor fitted with a metal blade. Allow mixture to cool slightly, about 5 minutes. Add the eggs 1 at a time, pulsing to thoroughly incorporate each egg into the dough before adding the next, then proceed with the rest of the recipe.

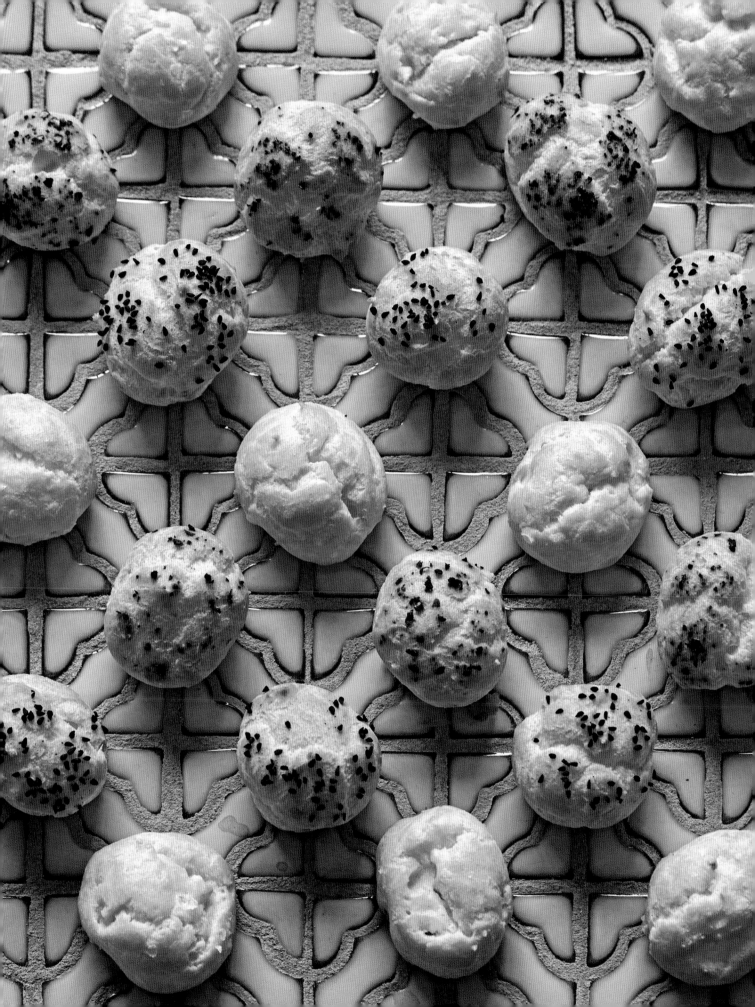

CHAPTER 4

SOUPS

SALT GOES WITH FOOD; MEASURE IT CAREFULLY.

— TURKISH PROVERB

ɪt's always tɪme foɾ soup

Preparing pasta for soup in Sakarya, in the Marmara region of the Black Sea coast

On a star-filled December night, we sit with our friends, sipping spoonfuls of hot soup, in a *corba lokantası*, or soup restaurant, in the city of Konya in central Anatolia. We've just come from the opening ceremony of the Whirling Dervishes Festival honoring the mystic poet Jelaluddin Rumi. At the performance, we were enthralled by the moving meditation where the dervishes' white coats were like clouds as they moved in slow, sweeping circles. Afterward at the restaurant, it is nearly midnight, but the tables around us are filled with other festival-goers fortifying themselves over bowls of soup, a staple of the typical Turkish diet.

In a room buzzing with animated conversation that steams the windows, the waiters hustle trays of aluminum condiment containers holding jars of dried mint, smoky red Aleppo pepper, black pepper and cumin to tables. Our friend Mahomut asks for extra lemon. We've adapted that Turkish taste for lemony soup in our own kitchens, in a rich broth thick with flavorful shredded chicken.

Soup recipes often carry with them years of tradition, like Bride's Soup, thick with lentils and bulgur, served to the bride as sustenance for her wedding night and life to come. We once spent an afternoon in a seaside village near Kekova dancing with the bride-to-be and other young women while the men, separated by partitions of colorful hand-woven blankets, sang songs of love. One strummed a saz and another beat a rhythm on a drum held between his knees, while the older married women gossiped, and from time to time joined in song as they stirred cauldrons of soup.

Soups are eaten in Turkey for breakfast, lunch and dinner. As in many kitchens around the world, including our own, leftover vegetables and meats from tonight's dinner often end up in tomorrow's soup pot. Inspired by thrift and creativity, our Chickpea Soup with Tomatoes and Spinach (page 91) is one of them.

Lentil soup with bulgur, mint and aleppo pepper

SERVES 6

1 cup (200 g) dried red lentils

2 cups (473 ml) water

1 tablespoon butter

1 teaspoon vegetable oil

1 teaspoon all-purpose flour

1 tablespoon dried mint

1 teaspoon Aleppo pepper

1 tablespoon tomato paste

1 tablespoon Turkish red pepper
   paste

6 cups (14 dL) vegetable or chicken
   stock

¼ cup (35 g) coarse bulgur wheat

2 to 4 teaspoons salt

Lemon wedges, for serving

Plain yogurt, for garnish

Chopped fresh mint, for garnish

a fateful error in a hotel reservation in Istanbul brought us to a meticulously restored nineteenth-century Ottoman-style hotel in Sultanahmet, near the Hagia Sophia, managed by a stylish Dutch chef who also ran a cooking school in the basement. In addition to savory sarmas stuffed with herb-infused rice and pomegranate-marinated kebabs, the Cordon Bleu–trained chef, with the help of her Turkish partner, taught us to thicken a classic Turkish red lentil soup with a spice-infused roux of Aleppo pepper and dried mint.

If you make this in advance, be aware that the bulgur will expand, making the soup thick. You may thin it with water as needed while reheating. This soup can serve as a main course with the addition of shredded cooked chicken, beef or lamb to the bottom of the bowl. Ladle the hot soup on top.

Put the lentils in a colander, rinse well and transfer to a 1½ quart (14 dL) pot. Add the water and set over medium heat, uncovered, and bring to a boil. Reduce the heat to low and simmer uncovered for 15 to 20 minutes, until the lentils begin to fall apart. They will change color from orange to yellow. Skim any foam from the surface during cooking. Add additional water if needed to keep the lentils submerged.

To make the soup, melt the butter with the vegetable oil in a large soup pot over a medium-low heat. Add the flour, stirring quickly to make a roux, and then stir in the dried mint and the Aleppo pepper.

Add the tomato paste and red pepper paste to the roux and stir vigorously for 3 to 4 minutes to incorporate the flavors.

Slowly whisk the broth into the roux. Add the lentils. Increase the heat to medium, stirring occasionally, until the soup starts to boil.

(RECIPE CONTINUES)

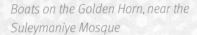
*Boats on the Golden Horn, near the
Suleymaniye Mosque*

Add the bulgur and reduce the heat to low. Simmer for 5 minutes, stirring occasionally to keep the soup from sticking to the bottom of the pot. Add salt to taste. Be generous, as lentils need a lot of salt to bring out their flavor. Turn off the heat, cover and let the soup sit for 5 to 10 minutes so that the bulgur can reconstitute. You can reheat the soup for a minute or two at low heat to bring the temperature back up.

Serve with lemon wedges. Garnish each bowl with a teaspoon of yogurt and fresh chopped mint.

Note: If red pepper paste is not available, increase the amount of tomato paste to 2 tablespoons and the Aleppo pepper to 1½ teaspoons.

THE SOLACE OF SOUP

The ferry crossing had been rough from Girne in northern Cyprus to Mersin on Turkey's southeastern coast. Waves cut across the boat's bow from every direction. To make matters worse, even though the sun shone clear and bright, it was November and the breeze was damp and chilly. By the time we disembarked, we were looking for lunch. Truth be told, there was only one thing we wanted: a soothing bowl of *mercimek çorbasi*, lentil soup.

We quickly found a restaurant in the bus station, a hole in the wall with Formica tables and florescent lighting, and ordered two bowls of lentil soup with ayran, a drink made of yogurt thinned with water and frothed to a milkshake-like consistency (see page 247).

A basket of warm pide arrived, followed by the tawny-red, perfectly smooth soup, drizzled with melted butter and infused with mildly spicy Aleppo pepper. The waiter watched us crumble in dried mint and add a squeeze of lemon. There are moments in life when everything is perfect, and this was one of them. We dipped our spoons into the creamy broth, brought the spoons to our lips and smiled.

Lentils of all hues, a Turkish pantry staple, are ready for the soup pot.

velvety red lentil soup with lemon

SERVES 6

1½ cups (300 g) dried red lentils

2 tablespoons butter or olive oil

1 teaspoon cumin

½ cup (55 g) roughly chopped
    sweet onion, such as Vidalia

½ cup (70 g) roughly chopped
    carrots

½ cup (50 g) roughly chopped
    celery, strings removed

1½ teaspoons salt, divided

6 cups (14 dL) vegetable, chicken or
    beef stock, or water

Plain yogurt, for garnish

Aleppo pepper, or hot or sweet
    paprika, for garnish

Dried mint or chopped fresh
    parsley, for garnish

Lemon wedges, for serving

Behind an unassuming façade, Sultanahmet Köftecesi's tables are filled with locals and tourists alike. While famous for its meat köfte, it is our go-to spot for pure and simple red lentil soup, especially after enjoying a Turkish bath at the nearby Çemberlitaş Hamamı. We like to sit at a marble table overlooking the Divanyolu, the Divine Road, watching students alighting from the tram on their way to Istanbul University and tourists ambling toward the Grand Bazaar. Alongside our bowls of soup, a basket—all too soon empty—brims with slices of soft fresh bread to dip into the broth. We do as the locals do, and squeeze fresh lemon juice into our soup, adding dried mint and Aleppo pepper to taste. At home, we make this soup often, and sometimes top it with rosemary- or thyme-flavored croutons.

Put the lentils in a colander, rinse well and set aside. Set a large pot over medium-low heat and add the butter. Swirl in the cumin and stir for 30 seconds until the cumin releases its perfume.

Add the onions, carrots, celery and 1 teaspoon of the salt. Sauté the vegetables for 10 minutes over low heat until the carrots and celery are soft and the onions are translucent but not brown. Slowly add the stock. Increase the heat to medium and bring to a boil.

Stir in the lentils and bring back to a boil. Give the mixture a stir and reduce heat to a simmer. Cover and cook for about 15 minutes, stirring occasionally, until the lentils are completely tender.

Turn off the heat and let the soup cool for a few minutes. Using an immersion blender, puree the soup until creamy. (It can also be pureed in batches in a blender or food processor.) Add the remaining ½ teaspoon salt, if needed.

Ladle the soup into serving bowls. Top with a spoonful of yogurt, sprinkle with Aleppo pepper and dried mint, and squeeze a lemon wedge on top.

mediterranean chicken soup with Lemon and cumin

SERVES 6 TO 8

This bright, creamy soup has two inspirations. The first was the flavorful carcass remaining after a meal of Cumin-Scented Roast Chicken Stuffed with Preserved Lemons and Thyme (page 190). The second is our love for the rich egg and lemon emulsion used to thicken soups throughout the Mediterranean region that's called *terviye* in Turkey, from the Arabic *tarbiya*, meaning to improve and refine. A handful of aromatic chopped dill reminds us of our Ottoman-Greek friends whose families planted the feathery herb in their gardens along the Aegean Coast. Serve with feta Gougères (page 75) and a crisp French Viognier or other fruit-forward white wine.

8 cups (19 dL) chicken stock

½ cup (105 g) uncooked orzo

1 cup (120 g) thinly sliced carrots

½ teaspoon cumin

1 cup (195 g) shredded cooked chicken

3 large eggs

3 tablespoons fresh lemon juice

1 to 2 teaspoons salt (depending upon the broth's saltiness)

¼ cup (13 g) chopped fresh dill, for garnish

1 lemon, cut into wedges, for serving

In a large soup pot, bring the stock to a boil. Add the orzo, carrots and cumin. Cook at a low boil for 5 minutes. Reduce the heat to a simmer and add the chicken. Simmer for 5 to 10 minutes, depending upon the size of the orzo, until it is cooked through and the carrots are tender.

Meanwhile, in a medium bowl, whisk the eggs until frothy. Slowly whisk in the lemon juice until the mixture is the consistency of thick cream. To temper the egg and lemon mixture before adding it to the soup, slowly whisk a ladleful of broth into the bowl.

Add the tempered egg and lemon mixture to the hot soup, whisking gently until the soup becomes creamy. Do not allow it to boil or the eggs will curdle. Add salt to taste, garnish with chopped dill and serve with lemon wedges.

DILLED YOGURT SOUP WITH CHICKPEAS AND RICE

SERVES 4 TO 6

Often served after sunset to break the fast during Ramadan, this immensely comforting soup is served warm. We first tasted it in Gaziantep, a city near the Syrian border that is a culinary epicenter of Turkey, located on a major ancient trading route from east to west. Traditionally, tiny chickpea-sized balls made from chickpea flour give the soup a tender bite. While this labor-intensive step of rolling tiny dumplings brings women together in the kitchen for hours, we achieve nearly the same result by using canned chickpeas, which have a softer texture than those cooked from dried beans. Serve this soup warm with a drizzle of red pepper butter and Sweet Potato Yufka (page 67).

FOR THE RICE
½ cup (90 g) basmati rice

¼ teaspoon kosher salt

FOR THE SOUP
1 cup (240 ml) plain yogurt

1 large egg yolk

2 tablespoons all-purpose flour

5 cups (12 dL) vegetable or chicken stock, divided

1 cup (220 g) canned chickpeas, drained

1 teaspoon kosher salt

1 tablespoon lemon juice

¼ cup (13 g) chopped dill, plus 1 tablespoon, for garnish

2 tablespoons butter, melted

1 teaspoon Aleppo pepper

Lemon wedges, for serving

In a small saucepan, combine the rice and salt with 1 cup (236 ml) water. Bring to a boil, stirring once. Reduce the heat to a simmer, cover and cook for 20 minutes until the water is absorbed. Set aside.

In a large heavy pot, whisk together the yogurt, egg yolk and flour. Turn the heat to medium and whisk in 4 cups of the stock. Bring the soup to a simmer and cook for 5 minutes, stirring occasionally, until it thickens to the consistency of cream. Do not let the mixture boil as it may curdle.

Stir in the rice and chickpeas. Add up to 1 more cup (236 ml) of stock to keep the soup creamy but not too thin and simmer for 10 minutes. Add the salt and lemon juice. Stir in the ¼ cup (13 g) of dill.

Mix together the melted butter and Aleppo pepper. Ladle the soup into serving bowls, drizzle with the hot pepper butter and garnish with the reserved tablespoon of chopped dill. Serve with lemon wedges on the side.

Adding olive oil to caçik with mint and parsley at a kitchen in Istanbul

THE CHICKPEA AND THE COOK

Sakir's sister Ipek motions us to help with the soup. She dips her hand into the wooden bowl, pinches off a bit of dough made from chickpea flour and rolls the mixture between thumb and forefinger into ovals that look like chickpeas.

"You'd think we could just put cooked chickpeas into the soup instead of going to all the trouble of grinding them into flour, mixing up dough and shaping it back into chickpeas," says Angie.

Ipek translates Angie's comments to her mother and aunt, whose faces show equal measures of horror and mirth. "Oh, but the texture is so much smoother this way," Ipek says, laughing. She was showing us how to mix hot broth into a bowl of yogurt so the yogurt won't curdle when the mixture is stirred back into the simmering soup. "It wouldn't be the same dish at all. We would never serve it like that."

Another auntie arrives and puts Joy in charge of boiling the chickpea dumplings. As the delicate yellow balls swirl in hot water, Joy thinks of a story by Jelaluddin Rumi, about a chickpea and a cook:

A cook is boiling chickpeas in a large cauldron when one of the chickpeas realizes he will soon be ladled into a bowl and eaten. Frightened, he tries to escape.

With the back of her spoon, the vigilant cook pushes the chickpea into the pot and says, "You think I'm torturing you, but I am not. I'm simply giving you flavor. You have lived in sunshine and grown from the earth, and now your journey continues. You will mingle with cinnamon and cumin and rice and meat and become the lovely vitality of a human being."

chickpea soup with tomatoes and spinach

SERVES 4 TO 6

On a June afternoon, Erkut, owner of a small locanta in Harbiye—home of one of the world's largest laurel groves—invited us into the kitchen to meet Seyval, his wife. She showed us how to make the excellent chickpea soup we'd just had for lunch. From a large picture window, beyond the cypress and laurel trees, we could see the road from Harbiye to the Syrian border, slipping over the mountain range like a golden sash. While Seyval softened chopped onions and celery in butter and oil, she told us that her grandparents had left Syria before she was born, and that her grandmother taught her how to make this soup with dried chickpeas—a family staple—spinach and tomatoes from the garden and a single dried bay leaf plucked from a garland hanging over the kitchen door. This soup brightens our tables year round. In colder months, we substitute canned plum tomatoes and serve it with a Cheese-Filled Bread Boat (page 64) for lunch or supper.

In a large heavy soup pot, melt the butter with the olive oil over medium heat. Add the onions and celery and cook until just softened, 3 to 4 minutes.

Stir in the Aleppo pepper, paprika, mint and cumin until the spices release their fragrance. Add the tomatoes and the broth and bring to a rapid boil. Reduce the heat to a simmer and add the bay leaf, carrots and potatoes. Simmer for 15 to 20 minutes until the vegetables are cooked.

Add the chickpeas, salt and pepper, and bring back to a simmer. Stir in the chopped spinach. As soon as the spinach wilts, garnish with parsley and serve with lemon wedges.

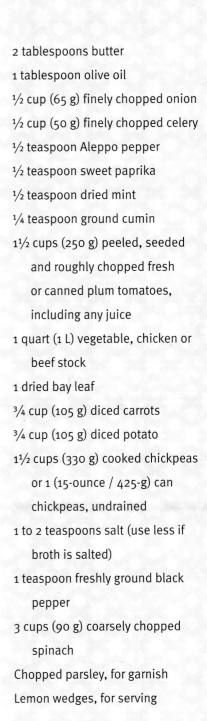

2 tablespoons butter

1 tablespoon olive oil

½ cup (65 g) finely chopped onion

½ cup (50 g) finely chopped celery

½ teaspoon Aleppo pepper

½ teaspoon sweet paprika

½ teaspoon dried mint

¼ teaspoon ground cumin

1½ cups (250 g) peeled, seeded and roughly chopped fresh or canned plum tomatoes, including any juice

1 quart (1 L) vegetable, chicken or beef stock

1 dried bay leaf

¾ cup (105 g) diced carrots

¾ cup (105 g) diced potato

1½ cups (330 g) cooked chickpeas or 1 (15-ounce / 425-g) can chickpeas, undrained

1 to 2 teaspoons salt (use less if broth is salted)

1 teaspoon freshly ground black pepper

3 cups (90 g) coarsely chopped spinach

Chopped parsley, for garnish

Lemon wedges, for serving

salads

THE SHARP KNIFE DOESN'T CUT ITS OWNER.
— *TURKISH PROVERB*

SaLaDs cLassic anD moDern

An oasis between dramatic tufa stone hills in the Rose Valley, Cappadocia

One afternoon, while hiking through the Rose Valley in Cappadocia, we found paradise. Apple trees hung heavy with fruit and grapes grew fat on well-tended vines. Further on, arugula and lettuces sprouted between rows of beets, their deep purple roots mounding in the soil next to squat cucumbers climbing up trellises. Above, we saw the remains of Greek homes and churches carved into soft volcanic tufa stone. We climbed further to get a better look at small dovecotes where bird droppings are gathered and used as fertilizer. A brief afternoon shower sent us scurrying into one of the cave houses, but it soon gave way to a sky so blue and warm, we could almost see the fruits and vegetables ripening in front of us.

Later, we stopped at a roadside restaurant and ordered a platter of orange slices topped with thinly sliced sweet onions drizzled with a buttery olive oil and studded with salt-cured olives (page 105).

Salads appear at nearly every meal in Turkey, and are frequently served as part of a meze table. We like to serve simple dishes, such as Melon with Feta, Mint and Pomegranate (page 106) or Grilled Romaine with Anchovy Vinaigrette and String Cheese (page 98), as starters. Peas and Carrots Salad with Artichoke Hearts (page 104), an Ottoman classic, is a celebration of spring, and a colorful addition to a luncheon or barbecue, especially during that brief season when fresh peas are available.

SHEPHERD'S SALAD

1 large cucumber, peeled, seeded and cut into 1-inch (25-mm) dice

2 large tomatoes, seeded and cut into 1-inch (25-mm) dice, juice reserved

½ cup (30 g) chopped scallion greens, coarsely chopped

½ to 1 teaspoon kosher salt

Juice of 1 large lemon

2 tablespoons extra-virgin olive oil

½ cup (25 g) coarsely chopped flat-leaf parsley

SERVES 4 TO 6

One summer the two of us managed a charmingly ramshackle hotel—its porch sagging under a cascade of overgrown magenta bougainvillea—called the Sun Pension in Kalkan, a tourist town on the Mediterranean. The tourist trade was slow that year, and we spent many afternoons taking the short ferry ride to Lycia Beach, a snack bar and swimming platform tucked into cliffs at the edge of the harbor. For lunch, we ate this refreshing salad every day, as did everyone around us, accompanied by amber bottles of Efes beer and French fries served with mustard.

Mingling ingredients that grow well and are widely available in Turkey—cucumbers, native to Asia, tomatoes from the Americas and scallions or green onions originating in western Europe—shepherd's salad is the country's most ubiquitous cold vegetable dish. Without the onion, it's a traditional Israeli salad; add some feta and olives, and it skews Greek. Despite the fact that it shows up with regularity as a meze or alongside a simple grilled fish, it never fails to refresh and beguile.

Put the cucumbers in a shallow bowl. Top with the tomatoes and their juice. Scatter the scallion greens over the tomatoes and add salt to taste.

The salad is best when eaten soon after it has been prepared. Just before serving, dress with lemon juice and olive oil, top with the chopped parsley and toss to combine.

Butter Lettuce Salad with Yogurt Dressing and Pomegranate

SERVES 4 TO 6

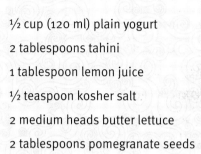

Native to Iran and northeastern Turkey, pomegranates are indispensable in the Turkish kitchen. The seeds are eaten out of hand, and fresh juice is sold from street carts during the fall when the fruits are in season. Rare is the salad or vegetable dish whose appeal is not heightened by the addition of juicy sweet and sour pomegranate seeds.

We especially enjoy this salad as a bright counterpoint to Lamb Kleftico (page 180), Roast Leg of Lamb with Rosemary, Garlic and Lemon (page 183) and Dill-Stuffed Whole Fish Baked in Salt (page 167).

½ cup (120 ml) plain yogurt

2 tablespoons tahini

1 tablespoon lemon juice

½ teaspoon kosher salt

2 medium heads butter lettuce

2 tablespoons pomegranate seeds

In a small bowl, whisk together the yogurt and tahini until smooth. Continue whisking while adding the lemon juice and salt. Taste to adjust seasonings.

Rinse the lettuce under cool water and dry thoroughly on a kitchen towel or in a salad spinner. Tear the leaves into bite-sized pieces, reserving 6 to 8 whole leaves. Line a bowl or serving plate with the whole lettuce leaves. Pile the remaining lettuce on top.

Drizzle the yogurt dressing over the lettuce and garnish with the pomegranate seeds.

Note: Pomegranates are in season in the United States from October through February. If you can't find the fresh fruit (or prepackaged pomegranate seeds), sprinkle ½ teaspoon ground sumac over the salad. It will provide a bit of color and a tart accent.

GRILLED ROMAINE WITH ANCHOVY VINAIGRETTE AND STRING CHEESE

SERVES 6

FOR THE ANCHOVY VINAIGRETTE

1 small clove garlic, minced

¼ cup (60 ml) lemon juice (from 1 or 2 lemons)

1 tablespoon anchovy paste

½ teaspoon kosher salt

⅔ cup (158 ml) extra-virgin olive oil

3 heads romaine lettuce

Vegetable oil, for brushing the grill

Flaky sea salt

Aleppo pepper

1 cup (113 g) shredded Armenian string cheese

Romaine lettuce has been cultivated for five thousand years and was known to the Romans as Cappadocian lettuce, named for the volcanic region of central Turkey with rich agricultural soil. Grilling adds a nice char to the greens while the tender interior leaves provide textural balance. Armenian string cheese (*tel banir*) from eastern Turkey is mild and salty, its fine strands available plain or studded with nigella seeds and then twisted into a braid. You may also find string cheese flavored with *mahleb*, an aromatic spice derived from a species of cherry, or with red pepper flakes. If using cheese with red pepper flakes, omit the Aleppo pepper.

In a small bowl, whisk together the garlic, lemon juice, anchovy paste and salt. Continue whisking while slowly adding the olive oil until the mixture is combined.

Pull the tough outer leaves from the lettuce heads. Trim the base of each head, making sure the remaining lettuce leaves stay attached to the stem. Cut each lettuce head in half lengthwise. Wash the lettuce and dry it well. Brush the cut sides with vegetable oil.

Heat a grill or grill pan to medium. Brush the grill with vegetable oil. Lay the lettuce, cut side down, on the grill and cook for 2 minutes. Turn the lettuce and cook the leafy side for 2 minutes. Turn the lettuce back to cut side and grill for 1 minute more.

Arrange the lettuce halves on a platter in a single layer. Drizzle the dressing over the lettuce, and sprinkle with flaky sea salt and Aleppo pepper. Scatter the string cheese evenly over the lettuce and serve.

aruguLa and fennel tulip salad with orange and radish

SERVES 4 TO 6

4 cups (80 g) arugula, rinsed and
   dried

1 medium navel orange

1 medium fennel bulb

2 medium radishes

2 tablespoons extra-virgin olive oil

1 small lemon, halved

1 teaspoon flaky sea salt, or to taste

Freshly ground black pepper

Native to central Asia and Persia, cultivated in Anatolia and prop-agated with unrivaled success by the Dutch, the lale, or tulip—particularly in the color red—is a symbol of love and beauty throughout Turkey. Live tulip plantings fill both public and private gardens and their image appears often on pottery, tiles and woven into carpets. While making this salad—which pairs bitter arugula with the licorice crunch of fennel, both native to Turkey—we noticed that if we cut a fennel bulb in half and cut those halves into thin slices, they reminded us of the feathery, light-filled tulips we've seen blooming in the gardens of Gülhane Park that links the Blue Mosque and the Hagia Sophia.

This composed salad has layers of color and taste, from the peppery arugula and radish to the sweet citrus and sharp fennel. It makes a beautiful first course, and can also accompany Circassian Chicken (page 186) or Rasim's Crispy Kalamar with Tarator Sauce (page 165).

Put the arugula in a wide, shallow serving bowl.

Use a sharp knife to remove the orange peel and white pith. Cut the orange in half lengthwise. Slice each half crosswise to create thin half-moons. Arrange the orange slices over the arugula in a garland near the rim of the serving plate, curved side out.

Remove the tops from the fennel bulb, reserving them for stock if desired, and slice off any stem. With a paring knife, cut out about ½ inch (13 mm) of the core from the bottom. If the outer layer of the fennel is tough, peel with a vegetable peeler. Slice the fennel bulb in half. Lay the bulb cut side down on a clean work surface and slice very thinly lengthwise. The fennel slices should look like lacy tulips. Arrange the fennel in slices over the arugula in a circle overlapping the orange segments.

Typically artful display of local produce at a fruit and vegetable market in Istanbul

Slice the radishes into thin disks and arrange them in a circle in the center of the salad.

Drizzle the olive oil over the salad, squeeze the lemon halves over it and season to taste with flaky sea salt and pepper.

101

tomato and walnut salad with pomegranate molasses

SERVES 4

½ cup (60 g) coarsely chopped
walnuts

3 medium red tomatoes, coarsely
chopped

1 tablespoon pomegranate
molasses

¼ cup (60 ml) extra-virgin olive oil

1 teaspoon kosher salt

½ teaspoon freshly ground black
pepper

½ cup (25 g) coarsely chopped flat-
leaf parsley

the walnut tree and its luscious, oil-rich fruit can be traced back to Mesopotamia as early as 2000 BCE. Today, Turkey is among the world's top producers of both tomatoes and walnuts. Turkish cooks have long understood that pairing sweet yet acidic tomatoes with buttery walnuts make a delicious marriage of cultures.

This salad works with any fresh tomatoes in season, but it's more decorative with a mix of heirloom tomatoes in different sizes, hues and flavors. Add it to your meze table or serve as a side dish.

Put the walnuts in a single layer in a medium skillet over moderate heat. Stir the nuts continuously for 2 to 3 minutes until they become fragrant and turn a rich golden-brown. Set aside to cool.

Cut the tomatoes into bite-sized pieces and put them in a nonreactive serving bowl. If there is any tomato juice left on the cutting board, add it to the bowl.

In a separate small bowl, whisk together the pomegranate molasses, olive oil, salt and pepper.

Add the walnuts and parsley to the tomatoes and gently fold to combine. Drizzle the dressing over the salad and gently toss again to mix. Finish with a few more grinds of black pepper, if desired.

peas and carrots salad with artichoke hearts

SERVES 6 TO 8

this is our take on a classic Turkish meze made year round, but especially when fresh peas and artichokes appear in the markets. Steamed carrots, chopped green onions, peas, cannellini beans and artichoke hearts are tossed with olive oil and lots of lemon juice and fresh dill for a flavorful and filling salad, best served warm or at room temperature.

1½ cups (210 g) peeled and diced carrots

½ cup (30 g) chopped scallions

8 fresh trimmed artichoke hearts, rubbed with lemon juice, or 1½ (9-ounce / 255-g packages) frozen artichoke hearts, thawed and sprinkled with lemon juice

1 cup (145 g) fresh or 1 cup (135 g) frozen peas

¾ cup (132 g) cooked cannellini beans, drained

¼ cup (12 g) chopped fresh dill, or 2 teaspoons dried

1 teaspoon kosher salt

Juice of 2 lemons

3 tablespoons extra-virgin olive oil

½ teaspoon flaky sea salt, plus more for serving

Lemon wedges, for serving

In a pan with a steamer basket, bring 2 inches (5 cm) of water to a boil. Add the carrots to the basket and steam for 3 minutes over medium heat. Add the chopped scallions and steam for 2 minutes more. Remove the basket from heat and reserve the cooking water. Put the carrots and scallions in a serving bowl.

Bring the water back to a boil with the steamer basket in place. Add the fresh or frozen artichoke hearts to the basket and turn the heat to medium. For fresh artichokes, steam for 15 to 20 minutes, depending upon their size, until tender but still firm. Steam frozen artichokes for 10 minutes. When tender, remove the steamer basket and rinse the artichokes under cold water. Pat dry and set aside.

Bring the reserved steaming water back to a boil, adding more water to reach 3 inches (75 mm). Drop the peas into the water. When the water returns to a boil, reduce the heat to a simmer and add the cannellini beans. Heat the peas and beans for 1 minute. Drain and add to the carrots and scallions.

If the artichoke hearts have stems, cut them off with a bit of the artichoke bottom and reserve for garnish. Cut the hearts in halves or quarters, depending upon the size of the artichokes, and add to the vegetables.

To finish the salad, add the dill, kosher salt and lemon juice and carefully mix to combine. Dress with the olive oil and sprinkle with flaky sea salt. Garnish with the reserved artichoke bottoms, stems up, if you have them. Serve with lemon wedges.

orange and red onion salad

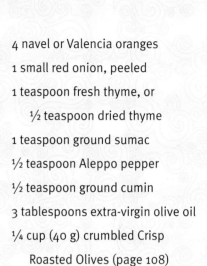

SERVES 6

One November, on a bus ride along Turkey's southeastern Mediterranean coast en route from Alanya to Cappadocia, we were surprised to pass an area with many orange groves, their trees heavy with fruit. With so many bags of oranges for sale at roadside stands, we wondered who would eat them all. We regretted having to miss the annual citrus festival in nearby Mersin the following week, where beauty queens ride atop floats in dresses made entirely of oranges. When we arrived in the heart of Cappadocia, we learned where many of those oranges are stored: in cellars dug into tufa stone to be eaten over the winter.

The formal Turkish word for sour orange and citrus, which first grew in Southeast Asia, is *narenciye*, a word derived from Sanskrit, meaning orange tree. Narenciye traveled to Spain and Portugal with Muslim traders and was grafted with the sweeter Seville and Valencia oranges. In the fifteenth century Portuguese traders then brought these oranges to Turkey, where they are now called *portakal*, from Portugal.

4 navel or Valencia oranges

1 small red onion, peeled

1 teaspoon fresh thyme, or
    ½ teaspoon dried thyme

1 teaspoon ground sumac

½ teaspoon Aleppo pepper

½ teaspoon ground cumin

3 tablespoons extra-virgin olive oil

¼ cup (40 g) crumbled Crisp
    Roasted Olives (page 108)

With a sharp knife, remove the peel and the white pith from each orange. Cut the orange in half lengthwise, and slice each half crosswise to create ¼-inch (6-mm) thick half-moons. Put the slices and any reserved juice in a serving bowl.

Cut the onion in half lengthwise then thinly slice each half and separate the slices. Add the onion to the oranges and mix gently.

Sprinkle the thyme, sumac, Aleppo pepper, and cumin over the onions and oranges. Drizzle on the olive oil and toss lightly. This salad is best if it sits at room temperature for 15 minutes before serving. Garnish with the roasted olives just before serving.

meLon with feta, mint and pomegranate

SERVES 4

Sweet honeydew melon provides a juicy counterpoint to briny crumbles of feta in this colorful salad. Melon salads are often served as a meze with rakı; this one is also a good first course for a light lunch or summer supper. The most important thing is to use a ripe, fragrant melon.

Slice the melon in half and scoop out the seeds. Cut the melon into 1-inch (25-mm) half-moon slices and remove the rind.

Layer the melon slices on a serving tray, overlapping if necessary. Sprinkle the feta over the melon. Garnish with the mint and pomegranate seeds.

In Turkey, the pomegranate harvest begins in late September.

1 ripe honeydew melon

4 ounces (75 g) crumbled feta
   cheese

½ cup (25 g) small fresh mint leaves

½ cup (75 g) pomegranate seeds

crisp roasted olives

MAKES 1 CUP (155 g)

Joy's husband, Fred (who never met an olive he doesn't love), devised this technique one afternoon when there was an overabundance of salt-cured olives in the kitchen. The crunchy olives turned out to be a delicious meze snack and a superb garnish when crushed and sprinkled on deviled eggs, omelets and salads. Once you make these, you'll want keep them around all the time, like we do.

An olive vendor at the market in Ayvalik, on the northwestern Aegean coast

1 cup (155 g) pitted black salt-cured olives

Heat the oven to 350°F (175°C) . Line a baking sheet with parchment or a Silpat. Spread the olives on the baking sheet and put in the oven. Bake for 40 minutes, turning once. Turn off the oven and let the olives continue to crisp while the oven cools, about 1 hour. Remove the olives from the oven. When they are completely cool and crisp, they're ready to eat.

Store in an airtight container for up to 1 month. If the olives lose their crispness, heat them in a 350°F (175°C) oven for 10 minutes.

white bean salad with Lemon

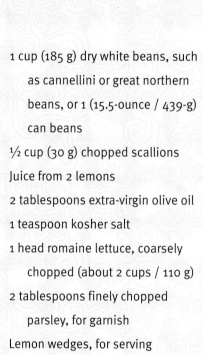

SERVES 6

At Sultanahmet Köftecisi restaurant, in business since 1920 and always full of hungry diners, we've been enjoying classic dishes since our first visit to Istanbul: warm bowls of lentil soup (page 86) and juicy köfte grilled with mildly hot peppers. We often order a plate of the restaurant's white bean salad, dressed with onion, parsley, lots of lemon juice and olive oil, and mop up the juices left in the salad bowl with the pillowy soft bread they serve mounded high in a plastic basket.

You can soak and cook your own beans or use drained and rinsed canned beans, as we do when we're in a hurry.

1 cup (185 g) dry white beans, such as cannellini or great northern beans, or 1 (15.5-ounce / 439-g) can beans

½ cup (30 g) chopped scallions

Juice from 2 lemons

2 tablespoons extra-virgin olive oil

1 teaspoon kosher salt

1 head romaine lettuce, coarsely chopped (about 2 cups / 110 g)

2 tablespoons finely chopped parsley, for garnish

Lemon wedges, for serving

If using dried beans, put the beans in a pot and cover with water. Soak overnight in a cool place. Drain the soaking water and add fresh water to cover the beans by 2 to 3 inches (5 to 7 cm). Over medium heat, bring the beans to a boil, then reduce the heat to a simmer. Cook, covered, for 1 to 1½ hours, until the beans are tender and cooked through but not breaking apart. Drain well.

If using canned beans, put in a small pot over medium heat until warmed through. In a mixing bowl, combine the warm beans, scallions, lemon juice, olive oil and salt. Gently mix and set aside for 15 minutes to let the flavors meld.

To serve, spread the lettuce on a serving platter and mound the beans on top. Scatter the parsley over the beans and place the lemon wedges around the platter.

RUSSIAN potato saLaD

this retro salad bound with mayonnaise was developed in the 1860s by a Belgian chef at the renowned Hermitage Restaurant in Moscow. By the early twentieth century, Russian salad had become popular in Istanbul, after Imperial Russians, fleeing the Bolsheviks, settled on the European side of the Bosporus. Traditional Russian dishes like this were always on the menu at the classic (now closed) Istanbul restaurant Rejans, a haunt of Kemal Atatürk, founder of the Turkish Republic.

Russian potato salad has many variations. This version is adapted from the recipe Joy's grandmother brought from eastern Germany. Store-bought mayonnaise will work perfectly well, but homemade mayonnaise elevates the flavor. Serve alongside Minted Lamb Burgers (page 177), or toss in a cup of chickpeas to make a hearty main-dish salad.

FOR THE DRESSING

¾ cup (170 g) mayonnaise

2 tablespoons sweet pickle relish

¼ cup (15 g) chopped scallions,
    white part and a bit of the green

¼ cup (13 g) chopped dill

1 teaspoon kosher salt

½ teaspoon freshly ground black
    pepper

FOR THE SALAD

3 medium carrots

3 medium Yukon gold potatoes

1 cup (145 g) fresh or 1 cup (135 g)
    frozen peas

4 large hard-boiled eggs, peeled

1 tablespoon chopped dill

½ teaspoon sweet paprika

To make the dressing, put the mayonnaise in a mixing bowl. Stir in the pickle relish, scallions, dill, salt and pepper.

Peel the carrots and potatoes and cut them into a ¾-inch dice. Bring 6 cups (1.4 L) of salted water to a boil in a large saucepan. Add the carrots and potatoes, stir once, reduce the heat and simmer for 10 minutes.

Add the peas, bring the water back to a boil and cook for 2 minutes more. Remove the vegetables from the heat and drain in a colander. Set aside to cool.

Coarsely chop 3 of the hard-boiled eggs, reserving 1 egg for garnish.

When the vegetables have cooled to room temperature, put them in a serving bowl and add the chopped eggs. Gently fold in the mayonnaise mixture to coat well. Add additional mayonnaise as needed, 1 tablespoon at a time. Be careful not to break up the ingredients.

Cut the remaining egg into quarters and arrange the egg wedges in the center of the salad. Sprinkle with the chopped dill and dust with paprika.

COCKTAILS WITH MATA HARI

Just after sunset, we hail a taxi at the Roman hippodrome and speed past Topkapi Palace, home of the Sultans, and over the Galata Bridge across the Golden Horn. The driver drops us off in Beyoglu near Rejans, a restaurant founded in 1921 by Russian Immigrants.

Caught up in the romance of the neighborhood, we stop for a drink at the Pera Palace Hotel where mystery writer Agatha Christie is said to have written her famous thriller, *Murder on the Orient Express*. The Pera Palace had a reputation for hosting some of the world's more interesting women including Dutch-born spy Mata Hari who, during World War I, kept a room at the Pera and passed secrets over cocktails.

Eyes follow us when we walk into the Pera's dark paneled bar. At a corner table, a group of businessmen drink scotch, smoke cigars, and exchange documents from leather briefcases. A woman in a fur-trimmed jacket perches on a barstool, running a fingertip around the rim of her martini glass. We settle into high-backed chairs under a tall window and order two rakıs.

manti, makarna and pilafs

SHE WHO KNOWS TO COOK RICE
WILL ALWAYS HAVE A FULL SPOON.
— *TURKISH PROVERB*

GRAINS OF THE FERTILE CRESCENT

Drying newly threshed wheat in the sun in Bogazkale, central Turkey

Our bus travels north from the city of Urfa through wheat fields along the western edge of the Fertile Crescent bordered by the Euphrates River. In the water-rich highlands of Anatolia, blessed with abundant rainfall, the earliest forms of wheat were domesticated along with pulses including peas, chickpeas and lentils.

We are on our way to the city of Van near the Iranian border, and to Mount Ararat where, according to the book of Genesis, the remains of Noah's ark lie buried beneath the snow. As the horizon undulates in tawny drifts, we think of the world's first communities who settled in this fertile land, harvesting and drying the seeds of many grasses. They turned those seeds into long-lasting, nutritious staples like bulgur and ground grain to be pressed into flatbreads made of water and flour. We further imagine how wheat traveled east across central Asia to China and back again, the basic combination of flour and water becoming pasta. When cut, filled, shaped and simmered in broth, that pasta (or *makarna*, in Turkish) becomes one of our all-time favorite dishes, the iconic dumplings called manti (page 116).

Another treasured Anatolian grain, rice—cooked into pilafs with lentils, peas and other legumes—was first cultivated in China and came with traders along the Silk Road to find a home in what was then Persia, as well as across the Arabian Sea to the Middle East. In fact, the Turkish word *pilav* comes from the Persian *polow*, and we've included a classic pilaf made with saffron, giving it a Turkish twist with the addition of chickpeas and mint (page 127).

There is a Turkish proverb that says, "No grain moves without a wind," but it's also true that great dishes move along trade routes in the minds, hearts and able hands of dedicated cooks, and they enter our cultures when we sit down and eat together.

Baked spinach, goat cheese and walnut manti

Long before Italian *nonnas* were pressing pasta dough into ravioli, the Uyghur Turks of central Asia were filling squares of thinly rolled wheat dough with spiced minced lamb or soft cheese to make the beloved dumplings called manti. The Turkish version is served with a spoonful of yogurt and a drizzle of melted butter swirled with Aleppo pepper.

While it is tempting (and possible) to substitute wonton or spring roll wrappers as we do in Weeknight Lamb Manti (page 121), nothing compares to the real thing made with freshly rolled egg dough. This is a fun dish to make with friends who can share the rolling, cutting and shaping of the pasta packets as well as the enjoyment at the table. The result is well worth the effort.

There are as many fillings for manti as there are cooks. Well-seasoned ground lamb is classic, but the spinach, goat cheese and walnut filling we use here is also deeply savory, as is the spicy chickpea variation that follows. This recipe makes enough dough and sauce for one of the fillings. To make both fillings, double the recipes for the dough and the sauce.

FOR THE FILLING

2 pounds (910 g) spinach, steamed and chopped (about 2½ cups / 390 g cooked)

½ cup (55 g) crumbled goat cheese

½ cup (60 g) finely chopped toasted walnuts

½ teaspoon nutmeg

¼ teaspoon freshly ground black pepper

FOR THE YOGURT TOPPING

2 cloves garlic, peeled

1 cup (240 ml) Greek yogurt

FOR THE TOMATO SAUCE

1 tablespoon butter

1 tablespoon olive oil

1 clove garlic, finely chopped

1 tablespoon finely chopped onion

1 small jalapeño pepper, seeded and finely chopped (optional)

1 teaspoon dried mint

1 teaspoon kosher salt

½ teaspoon freshly ground black pepper

2 cups (330 g) or 1 (16-ounce / 454 g) can crushed plum tomatoes, with their juice

Continued overleaf

Heat the oven to 375°F (190°C). Oil an ovenproof 9 by 13-inch (23 by 33-cm) baking dish or lasagna pan.

Make the filling: Squeeze the spinach to remove excess moisture and put in a bowl. Add the goat cheese, walnuts, nutmeg and pepper. Mix the ingredients until thoroughly combined. Taste to adjust seasonings and set aside.

Make the yogurt topping: Mash the garlic as finely as possible. Alternatively, put the cloves through a garlic press, or grate them on a fine grater. In a small bowl, blend the yogurt with the garlic, cover and keep it in a cool place until ready to serve.

Make the tomato sauce: In a medium skillet over low heat, melt the butter

(RECIPE CONTINUES)

1 recipe Egg Pasta Dough (page 120)

½ cup (120 ml) warm water

2 cups (473 ml) hot vegetable stock

½ cup (18 g) chopped parsley, for
  garnish

½ cup (20 g) chopped cilantro, for
  garnish

FILLING VARIATION

To make manti with chickpea
and Aleppo pepper filling, combine
3 cups (600 g) cooked chickpeas,
2 teaspoons Aleppo pepper,
2 teaspoons ground cumin and
2 teaspoons olive oil in a
medium bowl and mash by hand
with a fork or pulse in a food
processor into a coarse paste.
Add kosher salt to taste and
proceed with the recipe.

with the olive oil. Add the garlic, onions and jalapeño, if using. Sauté for 5 minutes, until the onions soften slightly. Add the mint, salt and pepper and sauté for 1 minute. Stir in the tomatoes and cook over medium heat until the mixture bubbles. Reduce heat to low and simmer for 10 to 15 minutes, stirring occasionally, until the sauce thickens. Keep the tomato sauce warm.

Make the manti: Put the pasta dough on a floured surface and divide it into thirds, keeping the unused pieces covered with a clean kitchen towel. Roll the first piece of dough into a rectangle about ⅛-inch (3-mm) thick. Cut the dough into approximately 2 by 2-inch (5 by 5-cm) squares. Set the warm water in a small bowl nearby.

Spoon ½ teaspoon of the filling into the center of each manti square. Using your fingers or a pastry brush, moisten the edges with the water. Seal the packets by pressing all 4 corners up and over the filling, pinching them closed along the seams and at the center. Each manti will look like a pyramid. Continue filling the packets until all the dough has been used. There will be approximately 100 packets. The manti can be frozen at this point (see Note).

Place the manti close together, side by side, in the prepared baking pan. If necessary, use an additional pan. If the manti don't fill the pan, simply place them as close together as possible. Put the pan(s) in the oven and bake for 15 minutes, uncovered, until the manti are golden brown.

While the manti bake, bring the vegetable stock to a boil in a medium saucepan, then remove from the heat.

Pour the warm stock into the baking pan to cover the manti halfway, ensuring that the manti are not fully submerged in the stock. Return the pan to the oven and bake the manti for 15 minutes more until the stock is almost completely absorbed. The tops will be crisp and golden brown.

Spoon the warm tomato sauce on a serving platter with a high rim. Transfer the baked manti to the platter, placing them evenly over the sauce. Dollop the yogurt sauce over the manti and garnish with the parsley and cilantro.

Note: To freeze the manti, place them in a single layer on a tray or plate and place in the freezer. When the manti are frozen, transfer them to a freezer storage bag. The manti can be frozen for up to 3 months. To bake, put in a single layer in a prepared baking dish. Let the manti thaw for 1 hour or until they come to room temperature. Bake as described in the recipe.

Forming manti is a skill passed down from one generation to the next.

LIGHT IN ORTAHISAR

We wake to see snowflakes falling from an eggshell-white sky. The flakes melt before touching the earth, leaving a damp chill. After breakfast of home-baked bread with butter, apricot jam, and local white cheese, Ahmet drives us to the village of Ortahisar to see an old Greek house that is for sale. Snow and ice linger in the shadows of houses built into a hill leading to the ruins of a castle perched at the top.

"Ortahisar has lovely light all year," says Ahmet, and we imagine summer holidays slicing cucumbers and chopping parsley from our garden for a salad.

Later, we stop in Avanos for lunch at a restaurant owned and run by local women where we're served steaming bowls of manti, hand-formed, pillow-soft dumplings stuffed with minced lamb and spices, smothered in a garlicky yogurt sauce and drizzled with warmed oil infused with red pepper. For the next blissful hour, we debate whether lentil soup or manti is our ultimate comfort food and decide they both win.

egg pasta dough

MAKES ABOUT 1 POUND (454 g) OF FRESH PASTA

In the Midwest United States, we grew up eating homemade egg noodles in soups and with gravy. Our first taste of Turkish manti made us realize how much wider the world of homemade pasta really is. This recipe includes a bit of olive oil to give the pasta a firm bite on its own and an excellent texture when making Baked Spinach, Goat Cheese and Walnut Manti (page 116).

2⅔ cups (330 g) unbleached all-purpose flour, plus more as needed

4 large eggs

2 tablespoons olive oil

To make the dough in a stand mixer, fit it with a dough hook and add the flour, eggs and olive oil to the work bowl. On low speed, mix until the dough forms a pale yellow ball. If using a food processor, pulse until the dough gathers into a ball. For both the mixer and processor, make sure all ingredients are incorporated and continue mixing for about 8 minutes until the dough becomes elastic.

To make the dough by hand, put the flour in a bowl or on a work surface and make a well in the center. Crack the eggs into the well and add the olive oil. With a fork or by hand, incorporate the flour into the egg mixture until the dough gathers together. Lightly flour a work surface. Gather the dough and knead it on the work surface for 8 minutes until the dough becomes elastic.

Wrap the dough in plastic wrap and let it rest for 1 hour at room temperature. Once rested, the dough is ready for use in a pasta machine, or to be rolled by hand for making manti.

weeknight Lamb manti

MAKES 36 MANTI

Several years ago, while researching our memoir, *Anatolian Days & Nights*, we stopped to have lunch with our friends Humyera and Rasim. Highly regarded writers and artists, both are excellent, generous Turkish cooks, but given their hectic schedules they have become adept at simplifying the traditional dishes they love to eat.

On that warm afternoon, Humyera made her delicious lamb manti, replacing labor-intensive fresh pasta with readily available wonton wrappers, which made an excellent substitute. The resilient dough makes these manti easy to cook in simmering water on the stovetop. While nothing compares to manti made with fresh pasta, when we're pressed for time, we no longer have to go without one of our favorite treats. Feel free to substitute ground beef or ground turkey for the lamb.

Line a baking sheet with parchment or brush it lightly with oil.

Make the meat filling: Grate the onion into a medium bowl using a box grater, making sure to capture all the juices. Add the lamb, parsley, salt and pepper. Mix thoroughly to combine.

Make the yogurt sauce: In a small saucepan, mix the yogurt and garlic. Gently heat to just below a simmer. Keep warm.

Make the butter sauce: In another small saucepan, melt the butter and swirl in the Aleppo pepper until the butter takes on a brick-red hue. Keep warm.

Set the water in a shallow bowl near the baking sheet. Unwrap the wonton wrappers and cover them with a clean kitchen towel to prevent them from drying out while you work. On a clean surface, lay out a few of the wonton sheets.

Spoon 1 teaspoon of filling into the center of each wonton square and moisten the edges with the water. Pull the 4 corners of the wrapper up and over the

(RECIPE CONTINUES)

FOR THE FILLING

1 medium onion

1 pound (454 g) ground lamb

1 teaspoon minced parsley

1 teaspoon kosher salt

½ teaspoon freshly ground black pepper

FOR THE YOGURT SAUCE

1 cup (240 ml) plain yogurt

1 large clove garlic, finely chopped

FOR THE BUTTER SAUCE

2 tablespoons butter

½ teaspoon Aleppo pepper, or
   ¼ teaspoon sweet paprika plus
   ¼ teaspoon hot paprika

FOR THE MANTI

½ cup (120 ml) lukewarm water

1 (12-ounce / 340-g) package square wonton wrappers

1 teaspoon dried mint, for garnish (optional)

filling. Press the edges together by pinching them closed along the seams up toward the center. Each manti will look like a pyramid.

Repeat with all the wonton wrappers, setting the finished packets on the baking sheet to dry slightly. Manti can be frozen for up to 1 month at this point.

To cook the manti, bring a large pot of water to boil. Slip the dumplings into the water in batches of 8 to 12. Bring the water back to a boil and lower to a vigorous simmer; cook for 9 minutes. Remove with a slotted spoon and drain well. Transfer to a shallow serving bowl or platter and cover the manti loosely to keep them warm. Repeat with remaining dumplings.

To serve, pour the warm yogurt sauce over the manti. Drizzle the warm butter sauce over the yogurt. Sprinkle with the dried mint if desired and serve.

ON THE ROAD TO ARARAT

Ishak Pasha fortress rises like a mirage through a late-afternoon haze, an amber and cream-colored castle we've seen in dreams and fairytales. We drive past a boy holding a switch broken from a tree branch, tending a few goats grazing amongst the rocky outcrops. Nearby, in the shade of an olive grove, a family sits on a blanket slicing a melon.

Gusts of hot wind swirl dust at our feet when we step from the car and enter the palace through the main gate. We pull scarves over our faces to shield noses and mouths from the whirling sand, and cross a courtyard large enough to hold the khan's army. The palace took more than one hundred years to complete and its kitchen had all the modern conveniences of its day, including heat and hot water.

mesopotamian mac and cheese

SERVES 6 TO 8

Mardin's limestone houses wind up and around a steep hillside like pearls threaded along a strand. On this particular late morning, after climbing nearly to the top, we caught our breath, entered a courtyard where a goat was munching on weeds while tethered to an iron bed frame and knocked on an ancient wooden door with a well-worn brass handle. An old woman welcomed us into her studio, her eyes appearing to be twice their actual size thanks to bottle-thick glasses.

An expert at painting religious folk-art designs on cloth, she showed us a series of images; the one that caught our fancy was a mermaid saint with tapered brown eyes, yellow flowing hair and a vermillion scaled tail: Atargatis, the great river goddess of Mesopotamia. But what also caught our attention were the hundreds of noodles, each the width of a pencil, drying on a wooden table and four chairs in the center of her studio.

Later, she invited us for lunch in the studio kitchen, dominated by a black cast-iron stove, and served us *eriste*, a Turkish dish with central Asian and Persian roots. She had baked the noodles in a creamy sauce, pungent with milk and cheese from the goat in the courtyard, and served it with glasses of mint tea.

We've created a milder version, giving an Anatolian twist to a childhood favorite. Elbow macaroni are enriched with feta and fontina in a rich béchamel, with crunch from an herbed breadcrumb and hazelnut topping. We like to serve this with Shepherd's Salad (page 96).

---

6 tablespoons (85 g) butter, divided, plus more for buttering the baking dish

¾ pound (240 g) elbow noodles

½ cup (50 g) breadcrumbs, or 2 slices of slightly stale bread processed into crumbs

¼ cup (20 g) ground hazelnuts or walnuts

1 tablespoon finely chopped parsley

1 tablespoon finely chopped chives

3 tablespoons all-purpose flour

1½ teaspoons white pepper

1 teaspoon kosher salt

2 cups (473 ml) milk

8 ounces (220 g) shredded fontina cheese

8 ounces (220 g) crumbled feta cheese

Heat the oven to 350°F (175°C). Butter a 9 by 9-inch (23 by 23-cm) baking dish.

Bring a large pot of salted water to boil over high heat. Add the elbow noodles and cook according to package directions, 8 to 10 minutes. Drain and return to the cooking pot.

Put the breadcrumbs in a food processor. Add the nuts, parsley, chives and 2 tablespoons of the butter. Pulse 2 or 3 times to combine. Set the mixture aside.

Melt the remaining 4 tablespoons of butter over moderate heat in a heavy saucepan. Gradually add the flour, stirring to form a roux. Do not let the butter brown. Add the pepper and salt and slowly whisk in the milk until heated but not boiling. With a spoon, stir in the fontina cheese until melted, then stir in the feta until it melts.

Remove from the heat and slowly pour the cheese sauce over the noodles, mixing to combine.

Pour the macaroni into the prepared baking dish and cover evenly with the breadcrumb topping. Bake for 25 to 35 minutes, until the cheese mixture is bubbling and the topping is browned. Let the dish rest for 5 to 10 minutes before serving.

armenian rice and vermicelli pilaf

at the beginning of the twentieth century, in the twilight of the Ottoman Empire, Turkey's Armenian population was forced to flee. A community of refugees, including Pailadzo Captanian, relocated to America and settled in San Francisco. In their adopted country, they continued to cook traditional Armenian dishes. When Captanian shared her recipe for a simple but pleasing pilaf of rice and thin pasta with her neighbors Tom and Lois DeDomenico (who happened to own a pasta company), the legendary "San Francisco treat" was born. The original inspiration for what was packaged as Rice-a-Roni is an elegant, comforting dish with roots in eastern Anatolia.

Serve this pilaf as a side dish with lamb chops, grilled chicken or any meat or vegetable kebab.

2 tablespoons butter

½ cup (50 g) angel hair (vermicelli) or thin spaghetti broken into ¼-inch (6-mm) pieces

1 cup (180 g) basmati rice

2½ cups (591 ml) chicken stock or water

1 teaspoon kosher salt

Melt the butter in a medium saucepan. When the butter begins to foam, add the vermicelli and stir until the noodles turn golden brown, releasing a nutty aroma. Add the rice and cook for 1 minute or until the rice becomes translucent.

Add the stock and salt to the rice and pasta, stir to combine and bring the mixture to a boil. Reduce the heat to a simmer and cover the pot. Cook for 20 minutes without opening the lid.

After 20 minutes, check to see that the rice and pasta have absorbed all the liquid. If not, cook 1 or 2 minutes more, making sure that the pilaf doesn't burn. Remove from the heat and drain any excess water. Let it rest for a few minutes before serving.

saffron rice pilaf with chickpeas and mint

SERVES 4

Inexpensive and easy to prepare, pilafs with chickpeas provide complete vegetarian protein. We've elevated this pilaf with saffron for golden color and subtle flavor. For a colorful, delicious meal, serve with Cumin-Scented Roast Chicken with Preserved Lemons and Thyme (page 190) and Mrs. Karaaslan's Beets (page 207).

1/8 teaspoon saffron

1/2 cup (120 ml) boiling water

3 tablespoons butter, divided

1 cup (180 g) basmati rice

1 teaspoon kosher salt

1 1/2 cups (354 ml) water

3/4 cup (165 g) cooked or canned chickpeas, drained

1 tablespoon fresh mint, or

1 teaspoon dried mint

Place the saffron in a small bowl and pour the boiling water over it. Set aside to steep for 10 minutes then strain, reserving the steeping liquid and discarding the saffron.

Over low heat, melt 2 tablespoons of butter in a medium heavy pan. Add the rice and stir to coat with the butter. Add the saffron water, salt and 1½ cups water. Bring to a boil, stir and reduce the heat to a simmer. Cover and cook for 20 minutes or until all the liquid has been absorbed and tiny holes form on the surface of the rice.

Melt the remaining 1 tablespoon of butter over low heat in a small saucepan. Add the chickpeas and heat just until they are warm and evenly coated with the butter. Stir the chickpeas and butter into the rice. Add the mint and serve.

BULGUR PILAF WITH FRESH HERBS

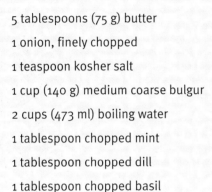

5 tablespoons (75 g) butter

1 onion, finely chopped

1 teaspoon kosher salt

1 cup (140 g) medium coarse bulgur

2 cups (473 ml) boiling water

1 tablespoon chopped mint

1 tablespoon chopped dill

1 tablespoon chopped basil

VARIATION

Rice Pilaf with Fresh Herbs
Following the instructions at
right, sauté the onion in
3 tablespoons butter, then add
1 cup (180 g) basmati rice and
2 cups (473 ml) boiling water.
Simmer, covered, for 20 minutes
before adding the herbs. Set
aside, covered, to rest for 15
minutes before serving.

SERVES 4 TO 6

With the first bite of this verdant pilaf we knew it would become a staple in our kitchens at home. In a class at the Culinary Institute in Istanbul, our teacher had artfully arranged a bouquet of mint, parsley, basil and dill in a tall glass and placed it in the middle of her demonstration table. She handed out knives and showed us how to stack the leaves into neat bundles, roll them lengthwise then chop them into a fine chiffonade. Then she showered them over a pot of steaming bulgur and their alluring aroma filled the room. No wonder we were smitten with this elemental dish.

Whole-grain bulgur, parboiled and dried, has been a staple in the Middle and Near East for six thousand years. It travels and stores well, and we can imagine camel caravans transporting sacks of it along trade routes. Bulgur also cooks quickly. We often serve this pilaf topped with Yogurt Dip with Cucumber and Mint (page 22) and Tomato and Walnut Salad with Pomegranate Molasses (page 102), for a light vegetarian supper. It is also compatible with Cumin-Scented Roast Chicken with Preserved Lemons and Thyme (page 190) and Mrs. Karaaslan's Beets (page 207). For the gluten intolerant, the recipe works perfectly with rice in place of bulgur (see Variation, left).

In a medium pot over moderate heat, melt the butter. Add the onions and sauté for 2 to 3 minutes. Stir in the salt.

Add the bulgur and stir to coat the grains completely with the butter. Remove the pan from the heat. Pour in the boiling water, cover with a lid and set aside for 15 minutes. When tiny holes form at the top of the bulgur, it's ready for the herbs.

Gently fold the mint, dill and basil into the bulgur. Place a clean tea towel or paper towel over the pot and replace the lid; the towel will absorb any excess moisture. Set the pilaf aside, covered, to rest for 10 minutes before serving.

tender green lentils with orzo and caramelized onions

SERVES 6

1 cup (200 g) French green lentils, rinsed and checked for stones

4 cups (946 ml) water, divided

1½ teaspoons kosher salt, divided

2 tablespoons olive oil

1 tablespoon butter

1 teaspoon ground cumin

¼ teaspoon cinnamon

2 medium sweet onions, halved and thinly sliced

½ teaspoon freshly ground black pepper

1 cup (210 g) orzo

¼ cup (35 g) toasted pine nuts, for garnish

1 teaspoon chopped rind from a preserved lemon, or 1 teaspoon finely chopped fresh lemon zest

1 tablespoon finely chopped parsley

Sweet, mellow onions slow-cooked to caramelization with cumin and cinnamon are the basis of this immensely satisfying dish. Lentils were one of the world's first domesticated crops and, according to archeological evidence, humans have been eating them for more than ten thousand years. In Turkey we would make this with the common large green lentil, but here at but here in the States we go for the small French variety, which hold their shape nicely. Serve with your favorite köfte or chicken dish, or on its own as a vegetarian main course.

Put the lentils in a medium saucepan with 2 cups (473 ml) water and ½ teaspoon of the salt. Bring to a boil, stir once and reduce the heat to a simmer. Cook, uncovered, for 20 to 30 minutes, until the lentils are tender but not mushy. Drain any excess water.

While the lentils cook, combine the oil and butter in a large skillet over medium-low heat. When the butter has melted, add the cumin and cinnamon and cook, stirring, for 1 minute until the spices release their fragrance. Add the onions and stir to coat with the spice mixture. Season with ½ teaspoon salt and the pepper. Reduce the heat to low and cook for 15 to 20 minutes, stirring occasionally, until the onions caramelize to dark brown.

Put 2 cups (473 ml) water and the remaining ½ teaspoon salt in a medium saucepan over high heat. Bring the water to a boil and add the orzo. Reduce the heat to low and let simmer, uncovered, for 5 to 8 minutes, stirring occasionally. Drain.

Put the pine nuts in a heavy skillet over medium heat. Cook, stirring occasionally, for 3 minutes or just until they begin to toast. Transfer the nuts to a small bowl and add the preserved lemons and parsley.

To finish the dish, stir the lentils and orzo into the pan with the caramelized onions and set over low heat until the mixture is warm but not hot. Taste to adjust seasonings. Transfer to a serving bowl and garnish with the pine nut mixture.

vegetarian stews and casseroles

WHEN YOU SIT AT THE DINNER, YOUR BELLY SINGS.
— *TURKISH PROVERB*

eggpLant and so much more

A market mosaic of the freshest herbs and vegetables in Kalkan

turkey is paradise for vegetarians. At every meal, from northern Cyprus in the Mediterranean Sea to the Kaçkar Mountains on the Black Sea and Bodrum on the Aegean, home cooks offer an array of vegetable dishes, usually prepared with olive or sunflower oil, as well as salads and pickles. Harvested from a nearby garden or purchased at the market from local farmers, vegetables have been baked in clay pots in communal ovens for thousands of years or layered into dishes such as moussaka (page 144) and (page 147).

The vegetable perhaps most synonymous with Turkey is *patli*, eggplant. Botanically classified as a fruit (actually, a berry), eggplant originated in southeastern Asia, and was first cultivated in Persia. It was unknown to the Greeks and Romans, but Arab traders, the Moors, brought it to Spain. Eggplant reached great popularity in Turkey in the Middle Ages, with many of the dishes originating in the royal Ottoman kitchens. In the late eighteenth century, Thomas Jefferson introduced the eggplant, a gift of the French king Louis XIV, into his garden at Monticello, Virginia.

It was a revelation to find leeks in a variety of preparations—stuffed, broiled and stewed—on menus, particularly in Istanbul and south along the eastern Aegean and Mediterranean coasts. Braised in tomato sauce, they are common fare in neighborhood locantas across the country. While no one has been able to definitively trace the origin of the leek, records show that it has been cultivated since at least 2100 BCE in the Mediterranean region, where it was thought to have restorative powers. The Assyrians of Mesopotamia believed eating leeks would keep their hair from turning gray.

melted Leeks in creamy tomato sauce

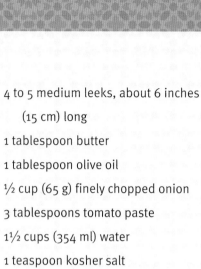

SERVES 4 TO 6

One of our favorite ways to cook leeks is in the Turkish manner, simmered in a simple tomato sauce bright with sumac. The leeks become silky and tender while their flesh absorbs the acid-sweet flavor of the sauce, enriched with yogurt just before serving. With some warm bread, this is an elegantly simple meze that it partners well with Classic fish, chicken or lamb too.

4 to 5 medium leeks, about 6 inches
   (15 cm) long

1 tablespoon butter

1 tablespoon olive oil

½ cup (65 g) finely chopped onion

3 tablespoons tomato paste

1½ cups (354 ml) water

1 teaspoon kosher salt

½ teaspoon freshly ground black
   pepper

½ teaspoon ground sumac

2 tablespoons plain yogurt

2 teaspoons lemon juice

2 tablespoons chopped dill, for
   garnish

Lemon wedges, for serving

To prepare the leeks, cut off the toughest green portion of the stem, leaving 1 to 2 inches (25 to 50 mm) of tender green leaves. Slice off the base including any attached roots, leaving the bulb intact. Slice the leeks lengthwise from base to stem. Rinse thoroughly under running water to remove any grit or sand.

Heat the butter and oil in a large skillet over medium heat. Add the onions and sauté for about 5 minutes, until soft but not brown. Stir in the tomato paste and water and bring to a simmer. Cook for 5 to 7 minutes until the sauce thickens to the consistency of light cream. If the mixture becomes too thick, thin with additional water 1 tablespoon at a time. Stir in the salt, pepper and sumac.

Put the leek halves into the tomato mixture, spooning the sauce evenly over them. Cover the pan and reduce the heat to low. Simmer for 30 to 40 minutes until the leeks are tender and easily pierced with a fork.

Remove the leeks from the pan and place on a warm serving plate. Cover and set aside while finishing the sauce.

Combine the yogurt and lemon juice in a bowl, then stir 1 tablespoon of the hot tomato sauce into the mixture to temper the yogurt. Stir the yogurt mixture back into the sauce in the pan. Season to taste with salt and pepper.

Pour the sauce over the leeks and sprinkle with the dill. Serve warm with the lemon wedges.

eggs cooked in sweet peppers, onions and tomatoes (menemen)

SERVES 4

"My friends are eager to meet you," says Faruk. On the streets of Trabzon, we pass fast food joints called Kebab Island and Chickenland and dart down an alley, stopping in front of a metal door next to a shoe shop. Faruk swings open the door and hurries us upstairs where we meet half-Canadian, half-Turkish Miriam, head teacher at the Grand Basic School of English, who insists that we join her and her students for lunch.

In a small galley kitchen, Miriam sautés tomatoes and peppers, their scent wafting into a nearby classroom where her students spread sheets of newspaper over a long table. Moments later, she emerges holding an over-sized cast-iron skillet steaming with one of our favorite dishes: *menemen*, a Turkish comfort food made with tomatoes, peppers and onions with eggs nestled in the sauce. One of the students, whose father is a baker, sets a three-foot-long loaf of bread on the table. "Please sit," says Miriam, tearing off pieces of bread and passing them around the table. The students dig in and we follow their lead, using the bread to break into the custardy yolks.

Menemen has become a regular weekend breakfast in our homes. We like to kick up the heat by adding finely chopped jalapeño pepper, but Aleppo or cayenne pepper work well, too. Serve this with Classic Puffed Pide Bread (page 62) for sopping up the juices.

2 red bell peppers

1 yellow or green bell pepper

1 medium onion

1 clove garlic, minced

2 tablespoons olive oil

1½ cups (250 g) chopped tomatoes with their juice, or 1 (14.5-ounce / 411-g) can diced tomatoes

1 teaspoon kosher salt

½ teaspoon freshly ground black pepper

½ teaspoon Aleppo pepper

½ cup (120 ml) water, divided

8 large eggs

Core and seed the peppers and thinly slice them lengthwise. Slice the onion in half and then into thin half moons.

Heat the olive oil in a large skillet over medium heat. Add the peppers, onions and garlic, if using. Stir to coat the vegetables with oil and sauté about 5 minutes, until wilted and beginning to brown.

Stir in the tomatoes, salt, black pepper and Aleppo pepper. Add ¼ cup (60 ml)

(RECIPE CONTINUES)

137

water and continue to cook for about 5 minutes, until the vegetables are soft and juices begin to simmer.

Reduce the heat to medium low. Use a spoon to create pockets in the vegetable mixture. Break an egg into a small bowl and then slide it into a pocket; repeat until all the eggs are in the skillet. Add up to ¼ cup (60 ml) of water if needed to steam the eggs. Cover the pan and cook until the egg whites are opaque but the yolks are still soft, 3 to 4 minutes depending upon preference.

Remove the skillet from the stove and set it on a trivet in the center of the table. Serve immediately with chunks of Classic Puffed Pide Bread (page 62).

Note: Two smaller skillets may be used. Divide the vegetables in half and cook 4 eggs in each skillet.

Black sea fondue (*kuymak*) with roasted winter vegetables

SERVES 4 TO 6

1 cup (135 g) cauliflower florets

1 cup (90 g) brussels sprouts, trimmed, large sprouts cut in half

2 large carrots, peeled and cut on the diagonal into 1½-inch (38-mm) pieces

3 tablespoons olive oil

½ teaspoon kosher salt

½ teaspoon sweet paprika

1 cup (110 g) fontina or mozzarella cheese, or ½ cup (55 g) fontina plus ½ cup (56 g) Armenian string cheese

½ cup (115 g / 1 stick) butter

½ cup (90 g) finely ground cornmeal

1½ cups (354 ml) water, or ½ cup (120 ml) white wine plus 1 cup (236 ml) water

½ teaspoon kosher salt

¼ teaspoon freshly grated nutmeg

a specialty of Turkey's Black Sea region, the sensuous fondue called *kuymak* is a dish best shared with friends. In fact, our friend Necat first served this to us on a cold evening in Trabzon while a north wind howled outside his high-rise apartment and the lights of ships and tankers blinked like stars on a nearly invisible sea.

At the stove, Necat stirred a mixture of butter and cornmeal. When a glistening layer of butter rose to the surface, he thinned the mixture with white wine and water, and added a shredded local cow's milk cheese similar to Armenian string cheese. The three of us sat at a card table in the living room, the pot of kuymak between us, with a bottle of Georgian wine and one of the Black Sea area's famous oversized loaves of airy bread for dipping.

Here at home, we relish kuymak as a comfort food, a polenta-esque fondue made with finely ground cornmeal. Encourage guests to spear the vegetables on forks and dip directly into the pot. As a side dish, divide the fondue among serving plates and arrange some of the vegetables on top.

Heat the oven to 450°F (232°C). Line a large baking sheet with parchment or a Silpat.

Put the cauliflower, brussels sprouts and carrots in a medium bowl. Toss the vegetables with the olive oil, salt and paprika to coat and spread them on the baking sheet in a single layer. Roast for 20 minutes, turning once for even browning.

While the vegetables are roasting, prepare the fondue. Cut the fontina into 2-inch (5-cm) cubes. If using string cheese, use your fingers to pull it apart into strips.

Over moderately high heat, melt the butter in a medium heavy saucepan. When the butter begins to foam, reduce the heat to low and whisk in the cornmeal. Stir while cooking for 3 minutes. Do not allow the mixture to brown.

(RECIPE CONTINUES)

Kuymak on the meze table in Artvin, near the Georgian border

Gradually whisk in the water, ½ cup (120 ml) at a time, and add the salt. Bring to a simmer and cook, stirring constantly with a wooden spoon, for 5 minutes. The mixture will release a layer of butter on top. Keep stirring the butter in and throughout the cornmeal.

Stir in the cheese, allowing it to melt into the buttery cornmeal. The mixture should lift from the spoon in creamy ribbons. When the cheese has melted, remove from the heat. Grate the nutmeg on top. Serve the fondue immediately from the pan with the roasted vegetables and crusty bread.

simmered eggplant with mushrooms and walnuts, ottoman style

SERVES 6

On a crisp fall day, we visited the Karyie Museum with its treasure trove of late Byzantine mosaics in Istanbul's Chora neighborhood. Afterward, we moved through history, so to speak, and sat down in a nearby Asitane restaurant to try a classic Ottoman dish, eggplants roasted with mushrooms. Inspired by the book *Bir Ziyafet Rehberi' (Guide to a Feast)* published in 1539, Asitane is one of the first restaurants to search for and recreate long-forgotten Ottoman recipes. Back in our own kitchens, we recreated the dish, adding cinnamon to the spice blend in a nod to Persian influences in the Ottoman kitchen. Walnuts add a textural counterpoint to the soft vegetables. Note that the eggplant is not peeled.

Serve warm with basmati rice or Rice Pilaf with Fresh Herbs (page 128) and Classic Puffed Pide Bread (page 62).

2 tablespoons butter, divided

1 teaspoon cumin

1 teaspoon sweet paprika

½ teaspoon cinnamon

1 teaspoon kosher salt

1½ pounds (682 g) globe eggplant, unpeeled, cut into 1-inch (25-mm) cubes (about 5 cups / 400 g)

1 cup (236 ml) vegetable stock or water

½ pound (58 g) cremini or baby portobello mushrooms, coarsely chopped

½ cup (60 g) coarsely chopped walnuts

¼ cup (9 g) chopped parsley

¼ cup (10 g) chopped basil

Freshly ground black pepper

Melt 1 tablespoon of the butter in a large pot over medium-high heat. Add the cumin, paprika, cinnamon and salt. Stir and cook until the spices release a sweet and nutty aroma, about 1 minute.

Add the eggplants, stir to coat with the spices and cook for 3 minutes, stirring frequently. Add the vegetable stock and bring to a boil.

Stir in the mushrooms and return the mixture to a boil. Reduce the heat to simmer, cover the pot and cook until the eggplants and mushrooms are tender and the sauce is silky, about 30 minutes. Check and stir the mixture occasionally, adding broth or water as necessary to maintain a saucelike coating.

Heat the remaining tablespoon of butter in a small pan over medium heat. Add the walnuts to the pan. Reduce the heat to low and toast, stirring occasionally, for 5 minutes, taking care not to let them burn. Add the walnuts to the vegetables along with the parsley and basil. Finish with a grind of black pepper.

spice-route moussaka

this vegetarian recipe is based on the classic Anatolian dish. Slices of roasted eggplant and cumin-spiced carrots are layered with a zesty tomato sauce and topped with creamy Béchamel Sauce with Parmesan Cheese (page 146). The vegetables and sauce can be made a day ahead then the dish can be assembled and baked to bubbling perfection.

Serve with a simple salad on the side, like Grilled Romaine with Anchovy Vinaigrette and String Cheese (page 98).

FOR THE VEGETABLES

2 to 3 Italian eggplants (about 3 pounds / 1,400 g), unpeeled

3 tablespoons kosher salt

¼ cup (60 ml) plus 2 tablespoons olive oil

2 pounds (910 g) large carrots

1 tablespoon ground cumin

FOR THE TOMATO SAUCE

1 tablespoon olive oil

1 medium onion, diced

2 cloves garlic, minced

¼ cup (44 g) finely chopped poblano pepper

1 (28-ounce / 794-g) can diced tomatoes with their juice

2 tablespoons tomato paste

½ cup (120 ml) dry white wine or water

½ teaspoon cinnamon

½ teaspoon Aleppo pepper

½ teaspoon kosher salt

½ teaspoon freshly ground black pepper

1 teaspoon sugar

¼ cup (13 g) chopped flat-leaf parsley

1 recipe Béchamel Sauce with Parmesan Cheese (page 146)

Heat the oven to 400°F (204°C) and line 2 large baking sheets with parchment. Cut the unpeeled eggplants crosswise into ½-inch (13-mm) thick slices. Place in layers in a large colander, sprinkling each layer with the salt. Let the eggplants sit for 30 to 60 minutes to release their liquid and prevent excess water in the finished casserole.

Rinse the eggplant slices with cold water and pat dry. Brush each side of the slices with ¼ cup (60 ml) olive oil and place on the prepared baking sheets in a single layer. Roast for 10 to 15 minutes, flip, and then roast for another 10 to 15 minutes until the eggplant is tender but not too soft. Remove the eggplants from baking sheets and set aside.

Line the baking sheets with fresh parchment. Peel and thinly slice the carrots on the diagonal to create large slices. Put on the baking sheets and add the 2 tablespoons of olive oil and the cumin. Toss to coat well and spread the carrots in a single layer on the prepared baking sheets. Roast the carrots for 30 minutes or until soft but not browned.

Reduce the oven temperature to 350°F (175°C).

To make the sauce: Put a heavy pot over medium-high heat and add the olive oil. Add the onions and sauté until soft, 3 to 4 minutes. Add the garlic and poblano peppers and sauté for 5 minutes more. Add the diced tomatoes and their juice, tomato paste and wine, then stir in the cinnamon, Aleppo pepper, salt and black pepper. Simmer for 30 minutes.

Add the sugar and parsley; season to taste and simmer for another 15 minutes. The sauce should be somewhat thick and chunky; if you prefer a smoother sauce, process with an immersion blender.

Make the Béchamel Sauce with Parmesan Cheese (recipe follows) and keep warm.

Evenly distribute a thin layer of the tomato sauce in the bottom of a 9 by 13-inch (23 by 33-cm) casserole dish. Place a third of the eggplant slices in a single layer over the sauce, and a third of the carrot slices on top of the eggplant. Spoon a third of the tomato sauce over the carrots. Repeat the layering process twice more with the remaining ingredients, ending with the tomato sauce.

Evenly spoon the béchamel sauce over the dish to cover and spread evenly across the top. Bake the moussaka for 1 hour, until the tomato sauce bubbles and top is slightly browned.

Let the moussaka sit for about 15 minutes before cutting.

Note: To make this dish vegan, omit the Béchamel Sauce with Parmesan Cheese and add 2 tomatoes, sliced. Layer on the top and sprinkle with ¼ cup (13 g) chopped parsley, then proceed with the recipe. For a meat version, sauté ¾ pound (340 g) ground lamb, beef or turkey in a medium saucepan to 10 to 15 minutes, until just cooked and nicely browned. Drain off any fat and stir the meat into the tomato sauce just before assembling the moussaka.

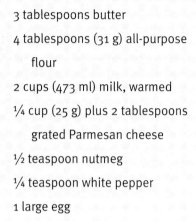

béchamel sauce with parmesan cheese

3 tablespoons butter

4 tablespoons (31 g) all-purpose
   flour

2 cups (473 ml) milk, warmed

¼ cup (25 g) plus 2 tablespoons
   grated Parmesan cheese

½ teaspoon nutmeg

¼ teaspoon white pepper

1 large egg

MAKES 2½ CUPS (591 ml)

Béchamel sauce first appeared in chef François Pierre La Varenne's eponymous cookbook in 1651. At the Topkapı Palace in Istanbul, a guide told us that béchamel was perfected during the reign of Sultan Suleiman the Magnificent, who ruled the Ottoman Empire during its Golden Age from 1494 to 1566, and was admired for his refined palate.

Over medium heat, melt the butter in a heavy saucepan. Add the flour and stir vigorously until smooth. Cook 2 to 3 more minutes, stirring continuously so the roux does not begin to brown.

Slowly add half the milk, stirring to avoid lumps. Add the remaining milk and bring the mixture to a boil. Reduce the heat and simmer for 2 minutes, stirring continuously. Remove the sauce from the heat and add the cheese, nutmeg and pepper.

In a small mixing bowl, lightly beat the egg. Pour ½ cup (120 ml) of the sauce into the beaten egg, stirring all the while to warm up the egg. Add the egg mixture to the saucepan and whisk until fully incorporated.

the imam fainted (imam bayildi)

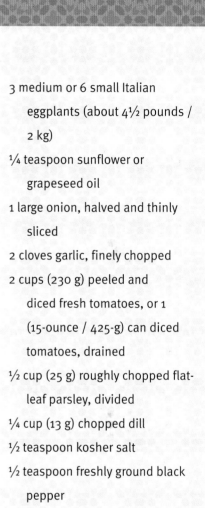

SERVES 6

First-time visitors to Istanbul walking past cafeteria-style restaurants on the touristic Divanyolu, or Divine Road, in the Sultanhamet district, or across the Golden Horn along ıstiklal Caddesi in Beyoglu, always comment on the trays of glistening eggplants stuffed with tomatoes and sliced onions in the windows. They're a Turkish comfort-food classic for good reason, and yield one of the very best leftovers we know. Serve alongside Bulgur Pilaf with Fresh Herbs (page 128).

3 medium or 6 small Italian eggplants (about 4½ pounds / 2 kg)

¼ teaspoon sunflower or grapeseed oil

1 large onion, halved and thinly sliced

2 cloves garlic, finely chopped

2 cups (230 g) peeled and diced fresh tomatoes, or 1 (15-ounce / 425-g) can diced tomatoes, drained

½ cup (25 g) roughly chopped flat-leaf parsley, divided

¼ cup (13 g) chopped dill

½ teaspoon kosher salt

½ teaspoon freshly ground black pepper

⅔ cup (158 ml) olive oil, divided

Juice of ½ lemon

½ teaspoon sugar

Flaky sea salt, for serving (optional)

Lemon wedges, for serving

Heat the oven to 350°F (175°C). Peel the eggplants in stripes, leaving on about half the skin. Slice the eggplants in half lengthwise, keeping the stems and base intact. If the eggplants have a lot of seeds, scoop some of them out.

Heat ⅓ cup (79 ml) olive oil in a large sauté pan over moderately high heat. Add the eggplants in 2 batches if necessary, turning to soften and brown on all sides. Add 1 tablespoon more oil if the pan becomes dry. Transfer to drain on a paper towel–lined platter.

Add more oil to coat the bottom of the pan. Add the onions and garlic and cook until soft, but not brown. Add the tomatoes, all but 1 tablespoon of the parsley, the dill, salt and pepper. Cook just until heated through, about 2 to 3 minutes.

Place the eggplant halves, cut side up, in a baking dish large enough to hold them all, squeezing them together if necessary. Spoon the onion-tomato mixture on top of each half. Pour the remaining ⅓ cup (79 ml) olive oil evenly over the eggplants and follow with the lemon juice. Sprinkle the sugar on top.

Cover the baking dish with foil and bake for about 1 hour. Check to see that the eggplants are soft. If not, continuing baking, checking at 5-minute intervals. If the eggplants have released too much liquid, remove the foil and bake for

(RECIPE CONTINUES)

another 10 to 15 minutes. The eggplants should be soft enough to cut with a fork.

Transfer the eggplants to a serving platter or individual plates and sprinkle with flaky sea salt, if desired, and the reserved tablespoon of parsley. Arrange the lemon wedges around the edges of the platter.

SO WHY DID THE IMAM FAINT?

According to Turkish legend, one day a lonely young Imam, or religious leader, named Hasif decided it was time to find a wife. Hasif was known to be a connoisseur of fine food. As a child, he frequented the spice bazaar with his mother to select the freshest pepper from Aleppo, the most fragrant mint from Antakya and the plumpest dried apricots from Malatya.

"You must meet Osman's daughter, İpek," said his friend Ahmet one afternoon. "Osman's caravans bring the finest olive oil from Lebanon to the market. They say that İpek is a better cook than her own mother."

İpek's father Osman was not a wealthy man. All he could offer for his daughter's dowry were twelve amphorae of olive oil to be delivered each year on her and Hasif's wedding anniversary. Hasif accepted the offer and married İpek. The marriage was a happy one.

Each Friday after final prayers, İpek served Hasif a special dish: small purple eggplant, cut in half and stuffed with chopped tomatoes, sliced

A time-honored method for preserving eggplants is to hang them in the sun.

onions and garlic, topped with fresh green herbs: parsley, dill and mint. Hasif loved it.

Shortly after their first anniversary, he sat down to dinner to find that İpek had made lamb kebabs and yogurt. "Where is my eggplant?" he asked.

İpek explained that the olive oil from her dowry was gone. Not a single drop was left. Her father had died during the past year and she would no longer receive her yearly allotment. She could still cook eggplant, but it would never taste the same.

Legend has it that the overwrought İmam fainted on the spot, or that he died from the shock. As the story was retold, the recipe traveled along the Silk Road to the kitchens at Topkapı Palace in Istanbul. From there, Imam Bayıldı would become famous throughout Turkey and the eastern Aegean. With its ingredients growing so abundantly in the region, it's no wonder that the legend of this dish is alive and well.

CHAPTER 8

fish and seafood

WITH AN INCH OF WATER, WE DREAM OF FISH.
— *TURKISH PROVERB*

BOUNTY of the seas

Setting out from Cunda Island in the Aegean, renowned for its seafood

With nearly 4,500 miles of coastline and Istanbul's famous Bosporus Strait connecting the Black Sea to the Sea of Marmara, and ultimately the Aegean, Turkey is a country that values its seafood. There we've enjoyed the most flavorful baked, grilled, steamed, fried and simmered fish we've had anywhere in the world.

Fishing is big business in Turkey. And still from humble wooden docks and fancy piers fishermen, and sometimes women, set out for the daily catch, often returning with enough glistening *barbunya* (red mullet), squid, octopus and shellfish to sell, but just as often for their own suppers.

Sea bass, *levrek*, mild and flaky, is one of the most popular Turkish fish. In fact, it has been in danger due to overfishing, prompting the growth of hatcheries along the Aegean coastline. Bluefish, *lüfer*, is also common, and the best are said to come from the Bosporus Strait. Year-round on the Black Sea, *hamsi*, sardines, are the catch of the day. Simply fried or grilled, they make the best finger food.

In fall, when bluefish begin their annual migration from the cool waters of the Black Sea toward the warm Aegean, we cross the Galata Bridge over the Golden Horn and watch fishermen in caps and women in headscarves leaning against the railing angling with rods, their buckets of minnows or containers of worms beside them. Vendors weave among us selling corn on the cob, simits and hot tea.

On the other side, at stands along the waterfront beneath the bridge, vendors call "*Balık ekmek!*" ("Fish sandwiches!") and "*Kalamar kızartma!*" ("Fried calamari!"). Just off İstiklal Boulevard in the covered Balık Pazarı (fish bazaar), we join local workers for lunch at one of our favorite *meyhanes* (pubs), where we share crisp, lightly battered, Mediterranean-caught calamari brightened with a squeeze of lemon and served, as delicious snacks so often are in Turkey, with a cool glass of rakı.

aegean tuna steak with thyme and oregano

SERVES 6

3 tablespoons dried thyme, divided

3 tablespoons dried oregano, divided

2 teaspoons grated lemon zest

2 pounds (910 g) tuna steak, cut into 6 (1-inch / 25-mm) thick portions

½ cup (120 ml) olive oil, plus more for brushing the skillet

¼ cup (60 ml) lemon juice

1 teaspoon kosher salt

Flaky sea salt

Lemon wedges, for serving

Wild-caught tuna fills an occasional yearning for the meaty texture of a thick beef steak. Here, sustainable albacore tuna is infused with the flavors of thyme and oregano, two heady, astringent herbs that grow wild along the rocky hillsides of Turkey's Aegean and Mediterranean coasts. In their dried forms, thyme and oregano (sometimes called wild marjoram)—both members of the mint family—add a particularly earthy savor. The flavor of both herbs is more intense at certain times of year, when many Turkish cooks harvest and dry them, hanging bunches from the kitchen ceiling to use in dishes like this.

Serve with Carrots with Whipped Feta and Preserved Lemon (page 200), and Roasted Potatoes with Bay Leaves (page 202).

In a shallow bowl large enough to hold the tuna steaks, combine 2½ tablespoons of the thyme, 2½ tablespoons of the oregano and the lemon zest. Add the tuna and turn to coat on all sides. Let the steaks marinate at room temperature for 15 minutes.

In a small bowl, whisk together the olive oil and lemon juice. Whisk in the remaining thyme, oregano and the salt.

Brush a large heavy skillet with olive oil and heat over high heat until a drop of water sizzles in the pan. Lay the tuna steaks in the pan in a single layer and cook for 4 minutes. Flip and cook for 4 minutes more, or until an instant-read thermometer registers 115°F (46°C) for medium rare. Transfer the steaks to a serving platter.

Pour the lemon juice mixture into the skillet and whisk over high heat until bubbling. Spoon the warm sauce over the tuna, season with flaky sea salt and serve with lemon wedges.

GRILLED TROUT, MOUNTAIN STYLE

SERVES 4 TO 6

friends brought us to their favorite restaurant tucked away in the Taurus Mountains above the rugged Lycian coast in southern Turkey. In the second millenium BCE, the Lycians established a tradition of independent city-states and a federal style of government that became the envy of the ancient world. They would have been familiar with the fish we ate that day, farmed and plucked from pristine ponds fed by mountain streams and grilled over open charcoal fires. We spent the afternoon drinking Efes beer, nibbling excellent fried potatoes and eating grilled trout with lemon, leaving only echoes of laughter in the air and a pile of bones on our empty plates. Serve the trout with a Cheese-Filled Bread Boat (page 64) and cold beer.

2 tablespoons olive oil, plus more
   for brushing
2 tablespoons coriander seeds
2 tablespoons fennel seeds
2 (1-pound / 454-g) whole trout,
   cleaned and gutted
4 sprigs fresh parsley
4 sprigs fresh oregano
4 sprigs fresh thyme (optional)
Lemon wedges, for serving

Heat a charcoal or gas grill to high. Using a sheet of heavy-duty aluminum foil make a pan that is large enough to hold the 2 fish and brush it with olive oil.

Put the coriander and fennel seeds in a small dry skillet and roast them until the seeds begin to pop and release their aromas, about 3 minutes. Cool and crush the seeds, then mix them with 2 tablespoons olive oil in a small bowl.

Rub the fish, inside and out, with the spice mixture. Divide the sprigs of parsley, oregano and thyme, if using, between the cavities of each trout. Slash the fish diagonally through the skin at 2-inch (5-cm) intervals on each side and place in the foil pan.

Place the pan on the grill, close the lid and cook over direct heat for 7 minutes. Gently turn the fish and grill for 7 minutes more, until it reaches an internal temperature of 120°F (49°C) to 125°F (52°C). Transfer the trout to a large serving platter. Fillet the trout and remove the spine before serving with the lemon wedges.

swordfish with Lemon, fennel and raki

SERVES 6

3 medium lemons

1 medium bulb fennel

1½ teaspoons kosher salt, divided

2 pounds (910 g) swordfish or
   halibut steak, divided into 2
   portions

¼ cup (60 ml) Turkish rakı, Greek
   ouzo or white wine

2 tablespoons chopped flat-leaf
   parsley

½ teaspoon flaky sea salt

Freshly ground black pepper, if
   desired

Lemon wedges, for serving

this recipe is inspired by evenings on the Mediterranean under starlit skies. The swordfish rests on a bed of fresh fennel. Thin disks of lemon are layered on top like golden scales, and a bit of rakı is poured in before the fish goes into the oven. Firm, flavorful halibut, native to the northern Atlantic and Pacific, is our go-to substitute for Aegean swordfish.

This makes a pleasing entrée accompanied by Sweet Potato Yukfa (page 67), Bulgur Pilaf with Fresh Herbs (page 128) and String Beans with Toasted Hazelnuts (page 206). When served at room temperature with small plates, it's an appetizer that pairs well with wine or cocktails.

Heat the oven to 375°F (190°C). Scrub the lemons and cut them into very thin slices, removing any seeds.

Trim the fennel of its green stalks and fronds (save for making vegetable stock). Cut the fennel bulb in half lengthwise. With a small knife, remove the solid core at the base. Put the fennel cut side down on a cutting board and slice thinly lengthwise.

Spread the fennel evenly across the bottom of a medium baking dish and sprinkle with ½ teaspoon of salt. Put the swordfish or halibut steaks on top of the fennel, then layer the lemon slices over the fish, overlapping the slices to look like scales.

Pour the rakı over the fish and sprinkle the remaining salt over the lemon slices. Cover the dish loosely with foil and bake for 15 to 20 minutes or until the flesh is just cooked through and the fennel is tender. Sprinkle with the parsley and sea salt, as well as black pepper if desired, and serve hot or at room temperature with lemon wedges.

sea bass baked in parchment

SERVES 6

This fish-for-company dish is a happy marriage of Anatolian flavors, including lemon, pistachio, dill and cinnamon. Cinnamon may seem an unusual spice to pair with fish, but it has been part of the Mediterranean pantry since at least the second century BCE. Here it contributes an exotic note reminiscent of a North African tagine. Lemony herbed butter adds festive richness to the austere fish, and a dusting of ground pistachios contributes crunch.

Baking in parchment or foil packets, as is done in many Turkish seafood restaurants, not only keeps fish moist and flavorful, it's also a dramatic way to serve any firm white fish on a bed of vegetables. As a bonus, clean-up is a snap.

6 tablespoons (85 g) butter, softened

1½ teaspoons finely chopped fresh dill, or 1 teaspoon dried dill

1½ teaspoons finely chopped parsley

½ teaspoon lemon zest

2 tablespoons olive oil

1 medium red onion, peeled and sliced into half-moons

2 cloves garlic, sliced

1 large red bell pepper, seeded and thinly sliced (1 cup / 90 g)

2 bay leaves

2 cups (230 g) peeled and diced plum tomatoes, or 1 (15-ounce / 425-g) can diced tomatoes, drained

2 cinnamon sticks, broken into 6 pieces

½ teaspoon sugar

1 teaspoon kosher salt

½ teaspoon freshly ground black pepper

2 pounds (910 g) meaty white fish such as swordfish, sea bass or halibut, about 1-inch (25-mm) thick, cut into 6 pieces

¼ cup (30 g) ground pistachios

Chopped fresh parsley, for garnish

Heat the oven to 350°F (175°C). Have ready a large baking sheet and 6 sheets of parchment or foil large enough to wrap each piece of fish.

In a small bowl, mash the butter with the dill, parsley and lemon zest to incorporate.

Heat the olive oil in a medium skillet over moderate heat. Add the onions, garlic, peppers and bay leaves and cook for about 5 minutes, until the vegetables have softened. Add the tomatoes, cinnamon, sugar, salt and pepper. Cook, stirring, until warmed through, then remove from the heat and discard the bay leaves.

Divide the vegetable mixture among the pieces of parchment, and add a piece of cinnamon stick to each. Pat the fish dry with paper towels and set 1 piece on top of the vegetables. Spread 1 tablespoon of the herb butter over the fish and sprinkle a little of the ground pistachios on top. Repeat with remaining fish to make 6 packets. Seal the packets by bringing both sides up and folding

(RECIPE CONTINUES)

The Golden Horn, spanned by the Galata Bridge whose metal steps we now climb, gives definition to a city that seems to float. Formed by the sweet water of two underground springs flowing toward the Sea of Marmara, the Golden Horn has sheltered ships for the Byzantines, Venetians, Genoese, Ottomans. It is an estuary rich with nutrients for many species of fish, including the glistening mullet sold with pride in the markets along its banks. —*J.E.S.*

them over once or twice at the top. Tuck the ends underneath. Make a 1-inch (25-mm) slit in each packet at the top near the fold so steam can escape, and transfer packets to the baking sheet.

Bake for 15 to 25 minutes depending upon the thickness of the fish, being careful not to overcook. The fish will continue to cook out of the oven.

Place each packet on a dinner plate and carefully cut open with a knife, taking care to avert your face from the hot steam. Garnish the fish with parsley.

Note: Both the herb butter and the vegetables in tomato sauce can be made 1 day ahead and stored, covered, in the refrigerator until ready to use.

shrimp in tomato and feta sauce (garides me feta)

SERVES 4 AS A MAIN DISH OR 6 TO 8 AS AN APPETIZER

The Greeks from Anatolia and along the Aegean coast know this classic dish as *garides me feta*. Make it in summer with ripe local tomatoes or with good-quality canned tomatoes out of season. For a casual supper with friends, we like to set the pan in the center of the table, Turkish style, and serve with plenty of fresh bread for dunking.

For a proper meal, serve with Bulgur Pilaf with Fresh Herbs (page 128) or basmati rice.

In a large frying pan over medium heat, warm the olive oil. Add the garlic and thyme to the pan and cook for 1 minute, stirring until the garlic is fragrant but not brown.

Stir in the tomatoes and any juices, salt and pepper. Break apart the tomatoes with the back of a spoon. Bring the mixture to a boil over medium-high heat then reduce the heat to a simmer. Cook the tomatoes until the sauce begins to thicken, about 8 minutes.

Stir the rakı into the tomato sauce and bring the heat back to medium-high until the sauce bubbles.

Arrange the shrimp in an even layer over the tomato sauce and cook for 3 minutes. Turn the shrimp and cook for 3 minutes more, until opaque and just firm to the touch. Add the crumbled feta. Turn off the heat, cover the pan and let sit for about 5 minutes to soften the cheese. Uncover and season with Aleppo pepper and flaky sea salt. Top with the chives, basil and parsley. To serve, divide the shrimp and sauce among 4 plates and garnish with lemon wedges.

1 tablespoon olive oil

2 cloves garlic, finely chopped

1 tablespoon fresh thyme leaves, or 1 teaspoon dried thyme

2 cups (230 g) roughly chopped plum tomatoes, or 1 (15-ounce / 425-g) can plum tomatoes with their juice

½ teaspoon kosher salt

½ teaspoon freshly ground black pepper

2 tablespoons Turkish rakı, Greek ouzo or white wine

1 pound (454 g) medium shrimp, peeled and deveined

8 ounces (150 g) feta cheese, crumbled

½ teaspoon Aleppo pepper

½ teaspoon flaky sea salt

1 tablespoon finely chopped chives

1 tablespoon roughly chopped basil

1 tablespoon roughly chopped flat-leaf parsley

Lemon wedges, for serving

marinated shrimp with orange zest and nigella seeds

SERVES 6

¾ cup (177 ml) olive oil

1 medium clove garlic, finely
chopped

2 teaspoons grated orange zest

2 teaspoons finely chopped fresh
oregano, or 1 scant teaspoon
dried oregano

1½ teaspoons nigella seeds

1½ teaspoons Aleppo pepper

1 teaspoon kosher salt

1½ pounds (781 g) medium shrimp,
deveined with shells and tails on

¼ cup (60 ml) orange juice

¼ teaspoon flaky sea salt

1 tablespoon chopped parsley

Orange wedges, for serving

Nigella, sometimes called black cumin, is grown in Turkey and is a prominent spice in the kitchens of its eastern regions. The seeds come from *Nigella sativa*, a plant native to Southwest Asia. *Nigella damascena*, the plant's domestic cousin, is a garden flower commonly known as love-in-a-mist, named for its lacy brackets surrounding a pale blue star-shaped flower. The seeds carry a faint hint of cooked onion and have a pleasantly peppery bite; while forthright, the taste is beguiling and easy to love. You may be familiar with them from Armenian string cheese or authentic New York City bialys.

Alternately, you may grill the shrimp over a hot flame or sauté them in the marinade in a pan. Serve with Grilled Flatbread (page 58) and Tomato and Walnut Salad with Pomegranate Molasses (page 102).

Pour the olive oil into a shallow nonreactive dish large enough to hold the shrimp in a single layer. Add the garlic, orange zest, oregano, nigella seeds, Aleppo pepper, and salt, and whisk to blend.

Add the shrimp to the marinade, turning to coat each piece. Cover and marinate at room temperature for 30 minutes or in the refrigerator for up to 6 hours. Bring the shrimp to room temperature before cooking.

Using a slotted spoon, transfer the shrimp to a plate. Pour the marinade into a large skillet. Heat over medium heat until the marinade starts to bubble.

To cook the shrimp on the stovetop, add the shrimp to the hot marinade and sauté 3 minutes on each side until the shrimp are pink and their flesh becomes opaque.

To cook the shrimp on the grill, prepare the marinade in the skillet and set aside. Place the shrimp in a grill basket. Cook over a medium-hot grill until the

(RECIPE CONTINUES)

AN EVENING ON THE BOSPORUS

The restaurant faces the slate-blue Bosporus. In summer, tables will be set outside under umbrellas for the crowds of sun seekers wandering by, but today the maitre'd leads us to a quiet corner inside the glass-front terrace where the owner delivers glasses of rakı.

"How's the red mullet tonight?" we ask, and the owner kisses his fingertips lightly, suggesting we order a whole fish baked in salt.

After serving mezes of white cheese, a cold eggplant dish called patlican, *cajik*–yogurt with crushed garlic and mint, the waiter brings the mullet in its salt crust. He cracks the crust open releasing the scent of the sea.

shrimp turn opaque, about 3 minutes per side. Add them to the hot marinade in the skillet.

Pour the orange juice over the shrimp. Sprinkle with flaky sea salt and garnish with the chopped parsley and orange wedges. Serve straight from the pan.

Rasim's crispy kalamar with tarator sauce

SERVES 6

Rasim, who has a home near the Black Sea, showed us his way of frying kalamar, or squid. Popular in Turkish seafood restaurants, crisp kalamar is often served with a tarator sauce—a delicious mayonnaise made with breadcrumbs and walnuts. Present the kalamar to your guests as Rasim does, piled high on a platter hand painted in shades of blue. It's wise to make extra, because the crisp fried rings and tentacles disappear fast. The sauce can be made a day or two ahead and kept covered in the refrigerator.

To make the sauce, put the walnuts in a dry skillet over medium-high heat and stir for about 5 minutes until toasted. Remove from the heat and, when cool enough to handle, transfer to a blender or food processor. Add the breadcrumbs, olive oil, garlic, lemon juice and salt. Blend on a low speed until smooth and creamy. Add water, 1 tablespoon at a time, if the sauce is too thick.

Heat the oven to warm and line a baking sheet with parchment.

In a medium bowl, combine the flour, salt, pepper, dried thyme and paprika.

Put the egg white into a bowl large enough to hold the calamari. Whisk until opaque and frothy. Add the squid to the bowl and toss to thoroughly coat.

Drain the squid in a colander and immediately add to the flour mixture, tossing to combine well. Set aside for 10 minutes. (The resting time is essential for crispy rings.)

Put the parchment-lined baking sheet in the warm oven. In a wok or a large heavy-bottomed pan with sides at least 3-inches (75-mm) high, heat the vegetable oil on high heat until it registers 360°F (182°C) on a deep-fry thermometer (see Note, page 166).

Lift the squid, 4 or 5 pieces at a time, from the flour, shaking off any excess, and carefully place them into the hot oil. Do not crowd the pan.

(RECIPE CONTINUES)

FOR THE SAUCE

1 cup (95 g) walnuts

½ cup (100 g) breadcrumbs soaked in water and drained

½ cup (118 ml) olive oil

2 cloves garlic, finely chopped

¼ cup (60 ml) lemon juice

½ teaspoon kosher salt

FOR THE KALAMAR

1 cup (160 g) rice flour

1 teaspoon kosher salt

1 teaspoon freshly ground white or black pepper

2 tablespoons dried thyme

1 tablespoon sweet paprika

1 large egg white

1 pound (454 g) squid, cut into ½-inch (13-mm) rings, tentacles left whole

2 cups (473 ml) vegetable oil

Lemons wedges, for serving

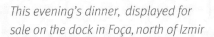

*This evening's dinner, displayed for
sale on the dock in Foça, north of Izmir*

Be careful not to let the temperature of the oil drop below 350°F (175°C).
Fry for 2 to 3 minutes, turning with tongs, until crisp and lightly browned.

Transfer the squid to the parchment-lined tray in the oven to keep warm.
Continue to fry the squid in batches, keeping each batch warm in the oven, until
all have been fried. Serve warm, with lemon wedges.

*Note: If you don't have a thermometer, drop a grain of rice into the oil. When the
rice pops back up and starts to fry, the oil is hot enough. Or dip the handle of a
wooden spoon into the oil. If bubbles rise around it, the oil is ready.*

DILL-stuffed WHOLE fISH baked IN saLt

SERVES 4 TO 6

In Turkey, the whole fish preferred for baking in salt is red mullet, also known as barbunya, but many other varieties can be cooked this way with equally delicious results. Joy's local fishmonger sometimes sells red mullet imported from Europe, but any smaller whole fish such as sea bass, red snapper and salmon work well. Serve with Shepherd's Salad (page 96) and rakı to drink.

2 tablespoons coriander seeds

2 tablespoons fennel seeds

2 (1-pound / 454-gram) whole trout,
    cleaned and gutted

½ bunch dill

3 large egg whites

5 cups (1,240 g) coarse kosher salt

5 tablespoons (74 ml) water

Lemon wedges, for serving

Heat the oven to 400°F (204°C). Line a baking sheet with foil.

In a small skillet, toast the coriander and fennel seeds until they begin to pop and release their aromas, about 3 minutes. Cool slightly and crush.

Rub the fish, inside and out, with the coriander and fennel seed mixture. Stuff half the dill inside each fish.

In a large bowl, whisk the egg whites until foamy. Pour in the salt and water and stir until the mixture becomes a thick paste with the texture of wet sand.

Make a salt bed for the fish by placing a little less than half of the salt mixture on the prepared baking sheet. Spread the salt in a layer about ¾-inch (19-mm) thick, 1 inch (25 mm) beyond wider than both fish, and 1 inch (25 mm) beyond their length.

Set the fish side by side on the salt bed. Mold the remaining salt mixture over the fish in a ¾-inch (19-mm) thick layer to cover and seal completely.

Bake for 20 minutes. To test for doneness, insert a sharp knife through the salt crust into the thickest section of fish. If the tip of the knife is warm, the fish is done. Or use an instant-read thermometer: the fish is done when the internal temperature reaches 120°F (49°C) to 125°F (52°C). The salt crust will be slightly browned.

Remove the fish from the oven and let it rest for 10 minutes. Firmly tap the crust over the fish with the back of a serving spoon to break the crust and peel it

(RECIPE CONTINUES)

The roaring seas and many a dark range of mountains lie between us.
— Homer, *The Iliad*

away. Remove the skin from the fish and place the top filet on a serving platter. Remove the spine and carefully transfer the bottom filet to the platter, leaving the skin and salt crust behind. Repeat with the second fish. Serve warm with plenty of lemon wedges.

ONE MAN'S FISH IS ANOTHER MAN'S DEER CHAT

As we take seats at one end of the horseshoe bar, Nusrat greets us with cheek kisses, a small copper bowl filled with dried, salted chickpeas and two glasses of rakı. From across the bar, Bekir, who owns an antique shop in the center of town, and Doğan, proprietor of a silver shop on the main street, wave hello.

The door opens and all eyes shift to Habib, who owns the big hotel in town. Dressed in khaki pants and a white linen shirt with a soft sweater draped over his shoulders, thick salt-and-pepper hair slightly tousled, he strolls in with an air of confident nonchalance.

He orders a drink and almost immediately is drawn into heated conversation with the other men. We don't understand much Turkish when it's spoken loud and fast like this. Habib shouts something at Bekir, who turns to Doğan, who yells back at Nusrat, arms flailing. Soon they're all talking at the same time, slapping rakı glasses on the bar for emphasis.

Habib sees us trying to keep up with the conversation. "We are only

An expressive sunburst of fresh sardines at a village market in Alaçatı, Izmir province

talking about fish," he says reassuringly. "Locally, there is a way of baking a whole fish in salt, but we disagree on the type of fish and the coarseness of the salt. Of course we all think the best recipes come from the region where we were born. And since I was born in İzmir near the Aegean, for me there is no fish better than red mullet stuffed with fresh dill and baked in medium coarse sea salt."

"*Hyer*, no," shouts Bekir, eavesdropping. "You must first coat the fish in red pepper paste, as we do in Gaziantep, and bake it in coarse salt."

Doğan, who comes from the Black Sea area, prefers *hamsi*, or sardines, coated in cornmeal and deep-fried in sunflower oil. There is silence for a moment as everyone ponders that thought.

"This is all *geyik muhebetti!*" says Nusrat suddenly. The men burst into laughter, diffusing the controversy.

"That literally means 'deer chat,'" explains Habib, noticing our confusion. "To talk, but to say nothing, like a herd of deer in a field."

CHAPTER 9

Lamb and chicken

THE HUNGRY MAN'S EYE ALWAYS FALLS ON THE PANTRY.
— *TURKISH PROVERB*

Savory and Aromatic Meats

In ten-thousand year-old Hasankeyf, one of the world's oldest continuously inhabited villages, we sit cross-legged beneath a reed roof on a platform suspended over the Tigris River, watching a group of boys swim and splash in the slow-moving current. Across the river, near the remnants of a twelfth-century bridge, a woman in shalwar pants and a red headscarf leads a single line of fat, woolly sheep down a rock-strewn slope toward the silt-green water.

So mesmerized are we that we startle when a young man sets before us plastic plates piled with fragrant pilaf and chunks of succulent slow-roasted lamb shoulder seasoned with rosemary and black pepper (page 183).

The image of sheep grazing in dun-colored fields beneath a burnt-white sky is one we will carry with us when we return home. In the neighboring villages, with *Eid al-Adha*, the Feast of the Sacrifice, a week away, we've seen the lone sheep or goat tied to a post being cared for and petted before meeting its fate.

Lamb and mutton are the most popular sources of meat in Turkey and have been grilled, stewed and braised for thousands of years. Our recipes for lamb chops marinated in pomegranate molasses (page 175) and *pekmez*, grape molasses (page 174) honor an Anatolian-Ottoman dish, lamb braised with tart plums. And while beef is still rare and expensive, it has become more available, especially in cities like Istanbul and Ankara. In recipes such as Minted Lamb Burgers (page 177), ground beef makes a fine substitute. Since Islam forbids eating pork, it's seldom eaten or sold in Turkey outside the remaining Christian neighborhoods and family-run businesses.

Chicken, another staple, is often tenderized with spiced yogurt marinades and paired with cumin, a versatile spice. One of the main ingredients of curry powder, in southeast Turkey cumin is found on the table as a condiment in small serving containers along with mint and Aleppo pepper.

In a restaurant kitchen in Sultanahmet, as at home, cooks begin by chopping onions.

Native to Iran, cumin was once used as currency and certainly traveled along ancient trading routes.

Traditional Circassian Chicken (page 186), paired with walnuts and walnut oil, has become of our favorites and is always a treat for guests.

mediterranean Lamb chops with pekmez

SERVES 6

Pekmez, or grape molasses, is a staple food in Turkish and Middle Eastern kitchens, where it is considered as much a nourishing tonic as a fruit preserve that finds its way into many different recipes. Pekmez is traditionally cooked in large kettles over an outdoor fire in autumn following the grape harvest. For breakfast, it is commonly swirled into tahini and eaten with bread. These chops may be grilled instead of pan-seared; in that case, make the sauce in a small saucepan. Serve with String Beans with Toasted Hazelnuts (page 206).

12 (1-inch / 25-mm) thick lamb chops (about 3 pounds / 1,400 g)

2 tablespoons olive oil

½ teaspoon kosher salt

½ teaspoon freshly ground black pepper

2 tablespoons butter

½ cup (70 g) finely chopped shallots

½ cup (120 ml) pekmez (grape molasses)

½ cup (120 ml) water

½ cup (120 ml) red wine

½ cup (75 g) seedless red grapes, halved

Put the lamb chops in a shallow dish in a single layer, drizzle with the olive oil, season with salt and pepper and turn to coat with the seasonings.

Heat a large heavy skillet over moderately high heat. Add the lamb chops, in batches if necessary, and cook on one side for 5 minutes, until lightly browned. Turn and cook for about 6 minutes more, or until the internal temperature reaches 140°F (60°C) to 145°F (63°C) for medium; the chops will continue to cook after being removed from the heat. Transfer to a serving platter and keep warm.

Return the skillet to moderate heat and add the butter. When the butter foams and bubbles, add the shallots and sauté for 5 minutes until they turn a light golden color. Stir in the pekmez and water and bring to a boil. Add the red wine. Bring the mixture back to a boil and reduce the heat to a simmer; let cook until reduced by half, about 2 minutes. The sauce should be the consistency of a light syrup. If it becomes too thick, add more water, 1 teaspoon at a time.

Remove from the heat and stir in the grape halves. Spoon the sauce over the lamb chops and serve.

Lamb chops with pomegranate sauce

SERVES 6

Nar ekşisi, or pomegranate molasses, is made from sweetened, reduced pomegranate juice. Although we keep store-bought bottles of this Turkish condiment in our pantries, it can be made at home. In a pinch, syrupy reduced balsamic vinegar may be used as a substitute. Here we've offset the pomegranate's tartness with Aleppo pepper and thyme for a flavorful finishing sauce. When sprinkled with juicy pomegranate seeds, this dish will brighten the dinner table. Serve with Arugula and Fennel Tulip Salad with Orange and Radish (page 100).

¼ cup (60 ml) pomegranate
   molasses, divided
1 tablespoon lemon juice
1 tablespoon tomato paste
½ teaspoon sugar
4 cloves garlic, crushed
2 teaspoons Aleppo pepper
1 teaspoon dried thyme
3 tablespoons olive oil
12 (1-inch / 25-mm) thick lamb
   chops (about 3 pounds/1,400 g)
Flaky sea salt
Freshly ground black pepper
1 teaspoon lemon zest
½ cup (75 g) pomegranate seeds,
   for garnish

In a bowl, combine 3 tablespoons of the pomegranate molasses, the lemon juice, tomato paste, sugar, garlic, Aleppo pepper and dried thyme, and mix well. Whisk in the olive oil.

In a shallow dish, lay the lamb chops in a single layer and rub the marinade on both sides of the chops. Leave the lamb to marinate, covered, at room temperature for 1 to 2 hours.

Heat the oven to 300°F (149°C). Remove the lamb chops from the marinade, reserving it to make the sauce.

In a heavy skillet over medium-high heat, sear the chops for 1 minute on each side and 30 seconds on the edges.

Set the skillet aside and transfer the lamb chops to an ovenproof roasting pan large enough to hold them in a single layer, or use two pans. Roast the chops in the oven, uncovered, for 10 to 15 minutes, or until the internal temperature reaches 140°F (60°C) to 145°F (63°C). Take care not to overcook. Remove the chops from the oven and let them rest uncovered for 5 minutes.

Return the skillet to the stovetop over medium heat. Add the reserved marinade and stir with a wooden spoon, scraping up all the browned bits.

(RECIPE CONTINUES)

A GRACIOUS MEAL AT HOME

Hülya spreads a white cloth embroidered with fine silk flowers on the floor. She orders Evren to set the cushions around it, and rushes back to the kitchen for plates, soup bowls, forks and napkins.

While we finish our tea, she gives the children their supper in the kitchen. Later, she returns, urging us to sit cross-legged on the floor while she ferries food from the kitchen. She must have spent all day preparing the feast: a traditional soup made with wheat berries and beef broth, topped with yogurt and hot red pepper flakes; sliced green beans sautéed with mint and tomato; and baby eggplants stuffed with minced lamb.

After dinner, ignoring Mahmut's protests, we give Hülya a break and clear the dishes. She leans against his shoulder and sips tea as we gather plates and bowls in our arms.

Add ½ cup (120 ml) of water and the remaining 1 tablespoon of pomegranate molasses. Stir to combine and bring the mixture to a boil. Reduce the heat to low and simmer for 3 to 4 minutes until the sauce thickens slightly. Season to taste with sea salt and pepper. Remove from the heat and stir in the lemon zest.

Place the lamb chops on a large serving platter and spoon on the sauce. Sprinkle with pomegranate seeds.

minted Lamb burgers

SERVES 6

Juicy grilled patties of seasoned ground meat are an integral part of the Turkish menu, and the super-deluxe gourmet burger shows no sign of losing its wild popularity in American bars and restaurants: two good reasons to try these savory herbed burgers of ground lamb topped with sautéed onions. While ground beef may be substituted, our friends and family love the flavor of lamb paired with mint in these burgers.

Toast the buns and top each burger with a thick slice of tomato, sautéed onions and a drizzle of Yogurt Dressing (page 97) or Kalkan Ketchup (page 46). Round out the barbecue with Russian Potato Salad (page 110).

4 cloves garlic

2 teaspoons kosher salt, divided

1½ pounds (781 g) ground lamb

2 large eggs, lightly beaten

1½ teaspoons freshly ground black pepper

⅓ cup (17 g) finely chopped mint, or 2 tablespoons dried mint

Yogurt Dressing (page 97)

1 tablespoon butter

1 tablespoon olive oil, plus more for brushing buns and burgers

1 large onion, cut in half and thinly sliced

6 sourdough rolls or hamburger buns

6 thick tomato slices

Fresh dill or mint sprigs, for garnish

Put the garlic on a cutting board and sprinkle with 1½ teaspoons salt. Mash the garlic into a paste and scrape into a mixing bowl. Add the ground lamb, eggs, black pepper and mint to the bowl and mix lightly to combine. With clean hands, form the meat into 6 patties, each about ¾-inch (19-mm) thick, and set them on a plate. Cover and refrigerate until ready to use. The patties can be made up to 24 hours ahead and taken out of the refrigerator 30 minutes before grilling.

Prepare the Yogurt Dressing and refrigerate until ready to serve. The sauce may be prepared up to 1 day in advance.

In a skillet over medium-low heat, melt the butter with the olive oil. Add the sliced onions and ½ teaspoon salt. Reduce the heat to low and cook for about 20 minutes, stirring occasionally, until the onions are lightly caramelized.

Heat a gas or charcoal grill to medium-high. Slice the rolls and brush the cut sides with olive oil. Place on the grill, cut side down, and toast them for 1 to 2 minutes.

Brush the burgers with olive oil. Set them on the grill for 3 minutes. Turn and

(RECIPE CONTINUES)

Out on the road through thyme-scented air
    and the haze of early afternoon,
I pass a grove of olive trees
    and a field of chamomile where goats graze.
Bells ring as they climb to higher ground.
    —Joy E. Stocke, *Cave of the Bear*

grill for about 7 minutes more until their centers are cooked through to 140°F (60°C) (for rare) to 145°F (63°C), depending on personal preference.

Place each burger on a roll and top with sautéed onions, sliced tomato and yogurt sauce. Garnish with dill.

Lamb *Kleftico* (Cypriot-style Lamb Shanks)

SERVES 6

6 lamb shanks (about 3 pounds / 1,400 g)

2 tablespoons fresh thyme

2 tablespoons fresh oregano

6 medium russet potatoes

6 medium carrots

6 cipollini onions, or 3 medium yellow onions

6 long, sweet-spicy peppers such as Anaheim or banana (optional)

2 tablespoons olive oil

2 cloves garlic, crushed

3 tablespoons tomato paste

¾ cup (177 ml) beef or chicken stock, or water

6 bay leaves

1 tablespoon kosher salt

2 cups (473 ml) dry red wine

1 teaspoon freshly ground black pepper

1 teaspoon flaky sea salt

¼ cup (9 g) roughly chopped parsley Lemon wedges, for serving

In Bellapais, in the mountains of Kyrenia in northern Cyprus, we met Deirdre Guthrie, proprietor of the guesthouse where we stayed. Deirdre, whose father was a composer and her mother an artist, grew up with the author Lawrence Durrell as a next-door neighbor. On Sundays, he would join Deirdre's family for slow-simmered, succulent Lamb Kleftico, arguably the national dish of Cyprus.

In Greek, *kleftico* means thieves, and the dish is named after the bandits and freedom fighters who lived in the Cypriot hills and forests. They would steal a lamb, bury it with smoldering coals from the previous evening's fire and let the meat cook slowly, undetected by passersby when they were away from camp.

This is Deirdre's recipe. She simmers the shanks in Maratheftiko, a dry wine from Cyprus, but a good California zinfandel, or a hearty cabernet or burgundy, works well too. The coastal hillsides of Cyprus and Turkey are lush with wild thyme and oregano, which give the dish robust flavor. It's not traditional, but we like to add a few mildly hot Anaheim or banana peppers for a spicy kick. This is a meal in a bowl. Serve with String Beans with Toasted Hazelnuts (page 206) and Grilled Flatbread (page 58).

Heat the oven to 325°F (163°C).

Put the lamb shanks in a bowl large enough to hold them (the shanks do not need to be in a single layer). If the lamb shanks have been in the refrigerator, let them come to room temperature. Add the thyme and oregano and toss to combine. Cover the bowl and set aside.

Peel the potatoes and cut in half, or in quarters if large. Peel and trim the carrots and cut in half lengthwise, then into quarters. Peel the cipollini onions and

(RECIPE CONTINUES)

leave them whole (if using yellow onions, cut into halves, or quarters if large). If using peppers, leave them whole.

Put the olive oil in a medium pan over moderate heat. Add the garlic and cook for about 30 seconds, just long enough for the garlic to sizzle slightly and exude its aroma. Add the tomato paste and stir to blend well. Add the stock and bring to a simmer, then remove from the heat.

Put the lamb shanks in a roasting pan large enough to hold them in a single layer. Tuck the potatoes, onions, carrots and bay leaves between the shanks. Pour the tomato sauce over the meat and vegetables. Top with the peppers, if using. Season with salt and pour the red wine over all.

Cover the roasting pan with foil and place in the oven. Roast the shanks for 2 to 2½ hours, checking once or twice and basting with the sauce. Remove from the oven when the meat is tender and falling off the bone.

To serve, arrange on a large platter and top with some of the sauce. Season with flaky sea salt and pepper and garnish with the chopped parsley. Serve with lemon wedges.

But that is what islands are for; they are places where different destinies can meet and intersect...
—Lawrence Durrell, *Bitter Lemons*

roast Leg of Lamb with rosemary, garlic and Lemon

SERVES 6 TO 8

This lamb takes us back to the fragrant hillsides above the Aegean. Roast lamb is a celebratory dish both here in the States, where it is often prepared for holidays, and in Turkey during the Feast of the Sacrifice, *Eid al-Adha*, which takes place seventy days after Ramadan to commemorate the prophet Abraham's willingness to sacrifice his son Isaac. Live lambs may be festooned with ribbons and henna, prayers are offered at the mosque and following the sacrifice, the meat is shared among the poor.

As our lamb roasts, lemon, white wine and two heads of roasted garlic meld with the pan juices to create a simple sauce. To set the mood, serve Bosporus Fizzes (page 246) for predinner cocktails, along with Anatolian Nut Mix (page 18). The lamb goes well with Arugula and Fennel Tulip Salad with Orange and Radish (page 100) and crusty bread on which to spread the roasted garlic.

1 (6-pound / 2,800-g) rolled
   boneless leg of lamb
¼ cup (20 g) fresh rosemary leaves,
   plus whole sprigs for garnish
1 tablespoon plus 1 teaspoon
   kosher salt
1 teaspoon freshly ground black
   pepper
3 heads garlic, one separated into
   cloves and peeled (about
   12 cloves)
3 lemons, cut into quarters, plus
   lemon wedges, for serving
¼ cup (60 ml) olive oil
2 cups (473 ml) white wine

Heat the oven to 400°F (204°C). Place the leg of lamb in a roasting pan. Finely chop the rosemary leaves with the kosher salt. Rub the rosemary salt over the leg of lamb and season with pepper.

Make deep slits, 1-inch (25-mm) wide and 1-inch (25-mm) long, evenly over the lamb equal to the number of garlic cloves, and insert a peeled clove into each slit.

Slice ¼ inch (6 mm) from the tops of the 2 whole garlic bulbs and remove some of the papery outer skin, leaving the bulbs intact. Set the bulbs in the pan, one on each side of the roast.

Add the quartered lemons to the roasting pan. Pour the olive oil and wine evenly over the lemons and the garlic, but not over the lamb.

Roast for 30 minutes, then reduce the oven temperature to 350°F (175°C) and roast for 45 to 60 minutes more, about 15 to 20 minutes per pound or until the

(RECIPE CONTINUES)

Whole lamb cooked for hours in a traditional pit oven anchors a celebratory meal.

internal temperature of the lamb reaches 135°F (57°C) to 140°F (60°C).

Remove the roast from the oven and let it rest for 15 minutes. The roast will continue to cook.

Meanwhile, remove the whole garlic bulbs from the pan, separate the cloves (leaving them in their skin) and set them aside. Pour the pan juices through a sieve into a small saucepan. Press on the lemons to release their juice. Keep the pan juices warm.

To serve, cut the roast into ½-inch (13-mm) thick slices and arrange on a platter. Spoon the pan juices over the lamb and garnish with rosemary sprigs. Pass the roasted garlic cloves to spread on rustic bread. Serve with lemon wedges.

sophisticated Lady's thighs
(sofistike kadinbudu)

SERVES 6 TO 8

It is said that *Kadinbudu*, spiced köfte, was created in the sixteenth-century Ottoman kitchens of the Topkapı Palace. They were shaped into oblong ovals, an homage to the assets of the women who lived in the sultan's harem. In tribute to these women, about whom we know so little, we created a modern version of the traditional recipe. Ask your butcher to bone the skin-on chicken thighs, or learn to do it yourself—it's easy. If you can find the Middle Eastern dried lemon peel, it adds extra complexity to the dish. Serve these with Mrs. Karaaslan's Beets (page 207) and Saffron Rice Pilaf with Chickpeas and Mint (page 127).

12 ounces (225 g) crumbled feta cheese

1½ teaspoons dried ground lemon, or 2 teaspoons fresh lemon zest

½ teaspoon freshly ground black pepper

1 cup (35 g) chopped parsley

12 boneless chicken thighs, skin on (about 3 pounds / 1,400 g)

Heat the oven to 350°F (175°C).

In a medium bowl, combine the feta with the lemon, black pepper and chopped parsley. Mix well.

Lay the chicken thighs, skin side down, on a work surface. Open and flatten slightly by hand.

To stuff the thighs, scoop 1 generous tablespoon of cheese filling into your hand and press it into an oval. Place the filling into the center of each chicken thigh. Fold the meat over the filling, right side then left, to create small packets.

Place the packets, seam side down, in a baking pan large enough to hold the thighs tightly together. It's okay if a bit of filling falls into the pan. If additional filling is left after stuffing the thighs, scatter it over the chicken.

Cover the pan with foil and bake for 15 minutes. Uncover and bake for 15 minutes more, until the internal temperature of the thighs reaches 165°F (74°C) and the skin has turned golden brown.

CIRCASSIAN CHICKEN
(POACHED CHICKEN WITH WALNUT SAUCE)

SERVES 6 TO 8

FOR THE CHICKEN

1½ medium onions, quartered

1 medium leek, white and green
    parts, coarsely chopped

1 large carrot, coarsely chopped

1 chicken (about 6 pounds / 2,800 g)

2 teaspoons kosher salt

3 cloves garlic, peeled

Small handful of cilantro or parsley

1 teaspoon black peppercorns

2 bay leaves

2 tablespoons butter

½ cup (65 g) finely chopped onion

FOR THE WALNUT SAUCE

3 slices bread, crusts removed

¼ cup (60 ml) milk

1 cup (95 g) shelled walnuts

4 cloves garlic, crushed

1 teaspoon ground coriander

1 teaspoon ground allspice

½ teaspoon freshly ground black
    pepper

½ teaspoon kosher salt

¼ cup (60 ml) walnut oil

1 teaspoon Aleppo pepper

¼ cup (10 g) chopped cilantro, for
    garnish

this celebratory dish of shredded poached chicken in walnut sauce, a particular favorite of ours, tastes rich and exotic. Following the classic Ottoman recipe, we tried making walnut oil by grinding the nuts with a mortar and pestle. The flavor was incomparable but it was very labor intensive and a messy process to obtain even a scant teaspoon of oil. We have settled on opening a fresh bottle of good-quality walnut oil from the supermarket, which works almost as well. Along with the oil, always use the freshest walnuts possible.

Circassian chicken makes wonderful use of a whole bird to feed a crowd, and the flavorful stock in which it's poached is used in the sauce made from fresh bread, walnuts and garlic. This dish owes its popularity in Turkey to the displaced people of Circassia, a mountainous region of Eurasia. In the late eighteenth and early nineteenth centuries, Russia invaded the Caucasus region between the Caspian and Black seas, forcing its inhabitants to flee into the Ottoman Empire. Turkey still has the largest Circassian population in the world, many of whom live along the Black Sea coast between Istanbul and Samsun. The physical beauty of the Circassian people has been noted throughout history.

MAKE THE CHICKEN: Put the quartered onions, leeks and carrots in a large stockpot. Remove and discard the neck and gizzards from chicken's cavity and set the chicken on top of the vegetables. Sprinkle the salt evenly over the chicken. Add the garlic, cilantro, peppercorns and bay leaves.

Add enough water to completely cover the chicken by 1 inch (25 mm). Bring to a boil, then reduce the heat and simmer, covered, for 1 hour. When the chicken has finished cooking, remove it from the broth and transfer it to a large bowl to cool.

Strain the chicken stock into a clean pot, pressing on the solids to extract as much liquid as possible. Reserve 1¾ cups (413 ml) of stock for this recipe and refrigerate or freeze the remaining stock for another use.

When the chicken is cool enough to handle, remove the skin and separate the meat from the bones. Shred the meat as finely as possible and set the shredded chicken aside. Discard the skin and carcass.

In a large skillet over medium heat, melt the butter. Add the chopped onions and sauté about 5 minutes, until soft and translucent. Add the shredded chicken and ¾ cup (177 ml) of the reserved chicken stock. Gently heat the mixture for about 10 minutes until the stock has evaporated. Spoon into a large bowl.

MAKE THE WALNUT SAUCE: Put the bread in a shallow dish. Cover with the milk and allow the slices to absorb it. In a food processor or blender, finely grind the walnuts with the garlic. Add the milk-soaked bread and pulse into a thick paste. Add ½ cup (120 ml) of the reserved chicken stock, the coriander, allspice, pepper and salt. Pulse to blend. Add more stock as necessary to create a smooth sauce the consistency of heavy cream.

Add the walnut sauce to the chicken mixture and toss gently to combine. Mound the chicken on a serving platter.

Just before serving, place a small pan over medium heat and warm the walnut oil until the surface ripples, about 1 minute. Add the Aleppo pepper and stir just until the pepper begins to darken, about 30 seconds more. Pour the pepper oil over the chicken and garnish with the chopped cilantro.

The Circassians are poor, and their daughters are beautiful.
—Voltaire, *Lettres philosophiques* (1733)

cumin-scented roast chicken with preserved Lemons and thyme

SERVES 6

It is no wonder that references to cumin are found in the Bible; it may well be one of the world's oldest spices. The name is thought to have derived from the Sumerian name, *gamun*.

When the aroma of preserved lemons, thyme and cumin perfumes your kitchen, it becomes, for a little while, a place of poetry. The bird emerges from the oven golden and crisp-skinned, and its flesh becomes fragrant, flavorful and tender to the bone. We will roast a chicken just to have just the leftover carcass from which to make soup the following day.

Serve with Armenian Rice and Vermicelli Pilaf (page 126) and String Beans with Toasted Hazelnuts (page 206).

FOR THE CHICKEN

½ cup (115 g / 1 stick) butter, softened

2 tablespoons ground cumin

1 (5- to 6-pound / 2,300- to 2,700-g) whole chicken

1 tablespoon kosher salt

1 small bunch thyme

2 sprigs mint

2 sprigs parsley

2 large preserved, or 3 small lemons, quartered

½ teaspoon grated lemon zest

FOR THE SAUCE

2 tablespoons pan drippings

1 tablespoon olive oil (optional)

1 tablespoon minced shallot

¼ cup (60 ml) white wine, or chicken or vegetable stock

¾ cup (177 ml) chicken or vegetable stock

1 tablespoon butter

1 tablespoon lemon juice

1 teaspoon chopped parsley

1 teaspoon chopped thyme

Kosher salt and freshly ground pepper

Heat the oven to 450°F (232°C).

Mix the softened butter with the ground cumin.

Pat the chicken dry with paper towels and set it in a large roasting pan, breast side up. Remove and discard the neck, liver and gizzards from the cavity. Sprinkle inside the chicken with salt and stuff it with the thyme, mint, parsley, preserved lemons and zest.

Carefully loosen skin all over the chicken, making sure to get under the drumsticks and into the cavities by the wings. Massage the cumin butter beneath the skin. It's okay to leave little lumps of butter. Tuck the wings beneath the breasts. With kitchen twine, tie the drumsticks together.

Roast the chicken in the oven, uncovered, for 20 minutes. Reduce the heat to 400°F (204°C) and continue roasting for 25 to 30 minutes more. When the chicken has been in the oven for a total of 45 to 50 minutes, insert an instant-read thermometer into the center of the breast. When the temperature reaches 165°F (74°C) and the juices run clear, the chicken is done. Remove it from the pan and set on a cutting board to rest for 15 minutes.

Meanwhile, prepare the sauce: Scrape any bits from the roasting pan and pour them with the drippings through a sieve into a small pan or bowl, pressing to capture all the flavor. Discard the solids.

Place 2 tablespoons of the drippings into a medium saucepan over medium-high heat. If necessary, add the olive oil to make a total of 2 tablespoons. Add the shallots and sauté until softened, about 3 minutes. Add the white wine and chicken stock and bring to a rapid simmer for 3 to 5 minutes until the mixture is reduced by half. Reduce the heat to low and whisk in the butter until incorporated. Whisk in the lemon juice. Stir in the parsley and thyme. Taste and add salt and pepper accordingly.

Cut the chicken into serving pieces. Transfer the chicken to a serving platter and top with the sauce.

yogurt-marinated grilled chicken

SERVES 4 TO 6

Using yogurt marinades to tenderize meat is a wise and ancient technique popular in India and the Middle East. The flavors of garlic, parsley and spices are absorbed by the chicken to create an exotic, succulent dish. Chicken can rest in the marinade refrigerated for at least one hour and up to twenty-four, so that the flavors penetrate but the meat doesn't get too soft. Serve with Classic Puffed Pide Bread (page 62) or Grilled Flatbread (page 58), and Shepherd's Salad (page 96).

1 tablespoon ground sumac

1 tablespoon dried mint

1 teaspoon smoked paprika

1 teaspoon sweet paprika

1 tablespoon kosher salt

1 teaspoon freshly ground black
    pepper

1 tablespoon lemon juice

2 tablespoons chopped basil

2 cloves garlic, minced

½ cup (110 g) chopped onion

2 tablespoons olive oil

2 cups (480 ml) plain yogurt

1 chicken (about 5 pounds / 2.300 g),
    cut into 8 pieces

In a bowl large enough to hold the chicken pieces, combine the sumac, mint, smoked and sweet paprika, salt, black pepper, lemon juice and basil. Add the garlic, onions and olive oil. Add the yogurt and stir to incorporate the spices.

Add the chicken pieces to the yogurt mixture and coat, pressing on the chicken to submerge the pieces in the marinade. Cover and marinate in the refrigerator for at least 1 hour and up to 24.

Heat a gas or charcoal grill to medium. Place the chicken pieces on the grill, skin side down, and discard the marinade. Grill the chicken for 20 minutes with the lid closed. Turn and cook another 10 minutes until the skin is golden. The chicken is fully cooked when the breasts reach 160°F (71°C) at their thickest part, and the legs and thighs reach 165°F (74°C), or when the juices run clear. Transfer to a platter and serve.

A TASTE OF THE PAST

Ghosts linger on the streets of Beyoglu. At the neighborhood's highest point, the Galata watchtower overlooks the Golden Horn, the horn is a shaped inlet off the Bosphorus in Istanbul. In the seventeenth century a Turk named Hazarfen Ahmed Celebi donned wings and jumped from the tower—the first successful flight over the Golden Horn.

History shifts at each corner, reminders of a time when merchants grouped together to sell a single product. On a street named Minare, shop owners display gleaming, gold-spiral minaret tops. On Balyoz, which means hammer, burly workers move among axes, pipes and kitchen hardware. Street names were also coined to reflect the traits of the shop proprietors: Gönül, willingness; Jurnal, informer; Acar, clever.

We spot the restaurant Rejans tucked into a dead-end alley in the old neighborhood of White Russian émigrés. Inside, little seems to have changed since the 1930s. Wood paneling, high ceilings, an orchestra loft and Art Nouveau wall sconces transport us back in time, as does the menu of buckwheat blini with Caspian caviar, borscht, and chicken Kiev. We're glad we got to experience it that night, because Rejans closed its doors for good in 2011.

CHAPTER 10

vegetables and side dishes

I PLANTED NO ONIONS; I TASTED NO FLAVOR.

— *TURKISH PROVERB*

IN SEARCH OF SOMETHING DELICIOUS

Produce vendor at rest in Balat, Istanbul's Jewish quarter since the Byzantine era

Turkey's first eating establishments were in caravansaries built a day's journey apart along the Silk Road, providing traders, pilgrims and travelers a place to rest, mingle and eat a restorative meal.

While there's been a long tradition of eateries catering to a noonday workforce, until recently most evening meals were eaten at home where everyone knew that mothers and grandmothers made the best food. We've gathered several recipes from them, including Mrs. Karaaslan's Beets (page 207), a simple, pleasing side dish or meze.

We love returning to Turkey for the food scene. While the categories of eating establishments can be confusing, once you know what each restaurant serves, your biggest challenge will be trying them all. In Turkey, locantas, or locandas (inns) are small restaurants with curated menus that serve a variety of dishes including fish, meat, vegetables and soups, especially at lunch. *Hazır yemek* (ready food) restaurants offer an array of prepared dishes such as Traditional Turkish Green Beans (page 198) slow-cooked in olive oil.

Balıkçısı (fish restaurants), their glass cases displaying fresh-caught barbunya, bluefish and shellfish, also have delicious sides to accompany the fish, including the inevitable but irresistible crisp potatoes (page 204) fried in sunflower or olive oil and seasoned with herbs. *Meyhanes* (from the Persian for wine house) are traditional tavern-like restaurants, serving wine, rakı and beer with meze and other dishes.

Kebapcesi (kebab restaurants) don't serve alcohol, so along with chicken or lamb kebabs (pages 47 and 49), we order a glass of cold yogurt-based ayran (page 247), a tangy, cool counterpoint to the often-spicy meat.

At times we splurge on lunch or dinner at restaurants like Matbah in the Sultanahmet district of Istanbul. It features authentic Ottoman dishes, some complex and others simple and elegant, like Sautéed Spinach with Yogurt and Paprika Oil (page 201).

And when in doubt, we eat from the food carts selling everything from pilafs to freshly dipped colorful candy on a stick that hardens before our eyes and gives a jolt of sugary pleasure as we contemplate our next meal.

traditional turkish green beans

SERVES 6

throughout Turkey, you will find green beans slow-cooked in olive oil and lemon juice in cafés, bus station restaurants and on home dinner tables. We've spent summer afternoons in a small village, gathered around a wooden table with the local women, stringing mounds of beans to go into a large communal pot for evening meals.

Unlike recipes that call for sautéing or steaming vegetables, these beans are cooked until they are very soft but not mushy. The key is to cook them in olive oil and add plenty of water. The beans can be served warm, at room temperature or even cold, and are traditionally offered as a separate course after the main dish and before dessert. They may be prepared up to a day ahead and brought to room temperature before serving.

¾ cup (85 g) coarsely chopped onion

2 cloves garlic, finely chopped

4 plum tomatoes, seeded and chopped, or 1 (15-ounce / 425-g) can diced tomatoes, drained

1 pound (454 g) green beans, trimmed and sliced in half lengthwise

1 cup (236 ml) olive oil

Juice of ½ lemon

1 teaspoon sugar

2 teaspoons kosher salt

In a medium pot, layer one-third of the onions, garlic, tomatoes and green beans, beginning with the onions and ending with the green beans. Repeat for 3 layers, ending with green beans on top.

Pour the olive oil over the vegetables. Add 1 cup (236 ml) water, the lemon juice, sugar and salt. Do not stir.

Bring the water to a boil, then reduce the heat to low and cook for 30 to 45 minutes, until the beans are tender but not mushy. Remove from the heat.

When the beans have cooled, drain off the liquid to prevent them from becoming mushy and transfer to a serving dish. Serve at room temperature.

carrots with whipped feta and preserved Lemon

SERVES 6

6 medium carrots (about 1
   pound / 454 g), cut into 3 by
   ½-inch (75 by 13-mm) sticks
¼ cup (60 ml) water
½ teaspoon kosher salt
1 tablespoon butter
½ cup (75 g) feta cheese, crumbled
1 cup (245 g) ricotta cheese
1 tablespoon lemon juice
1 tablespoon chopped preserved
   lemon

Most food historians agree that the wild carrot was first cultivated in the Himalaya-Hindu Kush region of Kashmir, Afghanistan and Turkestan in the second millennium BCE. Unlike the bright, sweet orange vegetable common today, these early carrots were a white or blackish purple and slightly bitter. It's commonly held that the enterprising, plant-breeding Dutch cultivated the orange carrot resembling the sweeter varieties familiar to us today.

There are many Turkish dishes that feature carrots, such as a traditional meze of shredded raw carrots with yogurt. Our recipe is a little different, but no less delectable. Serve with Aegean Tuna Steak with Thyme and Oregano (page 154) and Aegean Oven-Fried Potatoes (page 204), as a side dish for lamb chops or on a meze table.

Put the carrots in a large sauté pan with ¼ cup (59 ml) of water and the salt. Bring to a boil. Cover the pan, reduce the heat and cook the carrots over medium-low heat until tender but not mushy, about 7 minutes. Uncover and add the butter. Increase the heat to medium and sauté the carrots until all the water is evaporated.

In a mixing bowl, combine the feta and ricotta. Mash the cheeses together with a fork and add the lemon juice. Switch to a whisk to fully incorporate the cheeses and juice until light and airy. Fold in the preserved lemons.

Divide the whipped cheese mixture among 6 serving plates and top with the buttery carrots.

sautéed spinach with yogurt and paprika oil

SERVES 4 TO 6

his classic dish uses the Ottoman culinary technique of topping vegetables with cool yogurt sauce. Another common Turkish way to finish a vegetable or soup is to warm butter or oil in a small skillet with spices to release the flavors; in this recipe we use sweet paprika. The contrast between the warm sautéed spinach and cool spiced yogurt makes every bite a treat.

Delicious and beautiful, this recipe may be served as a meze or side dish with Sophisticated Lady's Thighs (page 185) and Sweet Potato Yufka (page 67).

¾ cup (180 ml) plain yogurt

1 medium clove garlic

1 teaspoon kosher salt, divided

2 tablespoons olive oil, divided

2 pounds (910 g) fresh spinach, well washed and coarsely chopped, or 2 pounds (910 g) fresh baby spinach

½ teaspoon freshly ground black pepper

¼ teaspoon nutmeg

¼ teaspoon sweet paprika

Spoon the yogurt into a small bowl. Finely chop the garlic with ½ teaspoon of the salt and add it to the yogurt. This may be prepared a day ahead and refrigerated until ready to use.

Warm 1 tablespoon of the olive oil over medium heat in a large skillet. Add the spinach and toss to coat with the oil. Add the remaining ½ teaspoon salt, the pepper and nutmeg. Cover the skillet and cook about 2 minutes if using baby spinach, and up to 4 minutes if using larger leaves, until the spinach has wilted. Add 2 tablespoons of water if the pan is too dry. When the spinach has cooked through, remove it from the heat. Drain any excess liquid.

Warm the remaining 1 tablespoon of olive oil in a small pan over medium heat. When the oil is warm, but not hot, add the paprika. Turn off heat and stir until blended.

To serve, put the spinach on a platter or in a shallow bowl, making a slight depression in the center. Spoon the yogurt sauce into the depression and drizzle the paprika oil over the yogurt.

ROASTED POTATOES WITH BAY LEAVES

SERVES 6

7 fresh bay leaves, or 5 dried bay
    leaves

6 tablespoons (85 g) butter

6 tablespoons (90 ml) olive oil

2 pounds (910 g) Yukon Gold or
    russet potatoes, cut into 2-inch
    (5-cm) chunks

1 teaspoon kosher salt

1 teaspoon freshly ground pepper

¼ cup (60 ml) lemon juice

Flaky sea salt

1 teaspoon ground sumac

Greek athletes were crowned with wreaths of laurels, and the Romans believed that the laurel tree could not be struck by lightning. Outside the city of Antioch are the ancient groves of Daphne, the mythological nymph whose father turned her into a laurel tree rather than allow her to be caught by Apollo. Walking through the grove one afternoon where we purchased bags of the dried leaves to bring home as souvenirs, we almost expected to see Daphne running among the three-foot-wide, smooth-barked trees.

The astringent flavor of bay leaves adds complexity to meats and stews and marries well with potatoes. Turkish bay leaves are often preferred among cooks, as they have a milder flavor than the more mentholated California variety. Sumac, a spice that grows wild in Turkey and all through the Middle East, adds a lemony, slightly sour taste.

Heat the oven to 350°F (175°C). Tear or break each bay leaf into 3 pieces.

Melt the butter and olive oil in a large ovenproof skillet over medium-high heat. When the butter is melted, add the potatoes and mix to thoroughly coat. Toss with the salt and pepper and add the bay leaves, tucking them in among the potatoes so they don't burn. Cover and bake for 20 minutes.

Uncover and bake for 20 to 25 minutes more, until the potatoes are tender and lightly browned. Serve in the skillet or transfer to a serving platter. Season with the lemon juice and flaky sea salt, and dust with ground sumac.

aeGean oven-fried potatoes

SERVES 4 TO 6

4 large russet potatoes (about
3 pounds / 1,400 g)

1 tablespoon sugar

¼ cup (60 ml) olive oil

1½ teaspoons kosher salt

1 tablespoon dried oregano

The summer we managed a guesthouse in Kalkan, after morning chores we would take a small ferry across the harbor and up a flight of stone steps to a café built into the cliffs that offered a sweeping view of the bay. There, over platters of crisp, hot French fries sprinkled with oregano salt, accompanied by glasses of cold beer, we would while away the afternoons.

As soon as the last fry had been eaten, another plate would appear. Though we knew the fries came from a huge bag of frozen potatoes in the café's walk-in freezer, we didn't really care, so happy were we with the company we kept, the sunshine and the cool blue waters where we swam. Back home in the States, we created our own version from fresh potatoes. These fries are fun as a snack with Kalkan Ketchup (page 46) and a frosty glass of beer. They also pair well with Dill-Stuffed Whole Fish Baked in Salt (page 167), Minted Lamb Burgers (page 177) or Chickpea Patties (page 44).

Heat the oven to 450°F (232°C). Line a large baking sheet with parchment or a Silpat.

Peel, trim and halve the potatoes lengthwise. Lay the cut sides down and cut lengthwise again into slabs about ¼-inch (6-mm) thick. Cut each of those slabs lengthwise again into generous ¼-inch (6-mm) sticks. Lengths can vary.

Place a colander in the sink or over a bowl. Put the potatoes in the colander and toss them with the sugar. Allow them to drain for 20 minutes. The sugar will draw out some of the moisture and help develop a crisp crust. Pat the potatoes dry with a clean kitchen towel or paper towel.

In a clean bowl, toss the potatoes with the olive oil. Combine the salt and oregano and add to the potatoes. Toss well to coat.

Put the potatoes on the baking sheet in a single layer and bake for 35 to 40 minutes, turning once midway through, until they are crisp and golden brown. Eat them while they're hot.

asparagus with walnuts and orange butter

SERVES 6

a s Turkish cooks know well, tender *kuşkonmaz*, or asparagus, are delicious when tossed with butter-toasted walnuts and slightly acidic orange juice. This makes an elegant side dish with Cumin-Scented Roast Chicken with Preserved Lemons and Thyme (page 190).

Cut the orange in half and then into quarters. Cut 1 of the quarters into slices and reserve the slices to garnish the finished dish.

In a large heavy pan, melt the butter over low heat. Add the walnuts and salt. Sauté for 5 to 7 minutes, until the walnuts are golden brown.

Increase the heat to medium and squeeze the juice from 2 of the orange sections over the walnuts, stirring to combine.

Turn the heat to medium-high and add the asparagus, turning to coat with the orange butter. Reduce the heat to low and cover the pan. Steam the asparagus for 5 minutes, until tender but still firm.

Remove the pan from the heat and squeeze the juice from the remaining orange quarter over the asparagus and walnuts. Toss 1 more time and turn onto a serving platter.

Season with flaky sea salt and garnish with the chopped parsley and reserved orange slices.

1 large orange

2 tablespoons butter

½ cup (60 g) coarsely chopped walnuts

½ teaspoon kosher salt

1½ pounds (781 g) thin asparagus, trimmed

Flaky sea salt

¼ cup (9 g) coarsely chopped parsley

String beans with toasted hazelnuts

SERVES 4

1 tablespoon butter

¼ cup (30 g) hazelnuts, roughly
    chopped

1 pound (454 g) string beans,
    trimmed

1 tablespoon water

½ teaspoon kosher salt

Freshly ground black pepper

Whenever green beans arrive in our local markets, we are reminded of the artfully displayed vegetables for sale in every neighborhood and village market throughout Turkey, including long, thin green beans piled high on wooden tables. Serve with baked or grilled fish, or slow-cooked lamb.

Melt the butter in a heavy skillet over medium-low heat. Add the hazelnuts and stir until they turn golden brown, about 5 minutes.

With a slotted spoon, transfer the toasted hazelnuts to a small bowl, leaving the butter in the skillet.

Add the string beans, 1 tablespoon of water and the salt to the skillet. Increase the heat to medium-high and cook, stirring frequently, until the water evaporates and the beans are tender but still crisp, about 5 minutes. Remove from the heat.

Add the hazelnuts and toss to combine. Transfer the beans to a serving bowl and season with a few grinds of black pepper.

MRS. KARAASLAN'S BEETS

SERVES 4 TO 6

as did we, our friend Sakir learned how to cook at his mother's knee. In his native Gaziantep in southeastern Turkey, it was common for children to spend time in the kitchen helping mothers and aunts prepare marinated beets, pilafs, Circassian chicken and melon salad. The women would pack their dishes into hampers and bring them to the *hamam*, the weekly communal bath, where they discussed the news of the day or the best matches between their marriageable children. This ancient ritual, which has largely fallen out of practice, was enjoyed among women for centuries.

At her home in Gazientep, we learned many of Sakir's mother's recipes. Her simple beet pickle, which we serve often at our meze and dinner tables, is the one that most reminds us of our friendship.

4 to 5 medium beets, cleaned and
   trimmed
½ cup (120 ml) canola or sunflower
   oil
¼ cup (60 ml) distilled white
   vinegar
1 tablespoon chopped shallot
1 teaspoon kosher salt, plus more to
   taste if needed
½ teaspoon sugar
½ teaspoon freshly ground black
   pepper
¼ cup (9 g) finely chopped parsley

Heat the oven to 375°F (190°C). Line a baking sheet with parchment, leaving enough overlap to cover the beets while roasting.

Cut each beet in half. Lay them cut side down on the baking sheet, cover with the parchment and seal and bake for 45 minutes or until tender. Set aside to cool slightly, about 10 minutes.

In a small bowl, combine the oil, vinegar, shallots, salt, sugar and black pepper. Whisk to combine.

When beets are cool enough to the handle, peel and cut them into bite-sized pieces and put into a serving bowl. Add the dressing and toss to coat. Garnish with the chopped parsley.

The beets may be prepared a day ahead and refrigerated overnight in a covered bowl.

Dessert: puddings, pastry and more

IF IT GOES IN WITH MILK, IT COMES OUT WITH SOUL.
— *TURKISH PROVERB*

sweets and traditions

A tower of sweets tempts on Istiklal Avenue in Istanbul's Taksim district

Most first-time visitors to Turkey are already familiar with two famous desserts: jewel-like squares of Turkish delight, or *lokum*, and flaky, nut-filled baklava. Both delicious treats can be purchased fresh from cases at confectioneries or baklava shops, where they come packed in pretty boxes and make wonderful gifts. Tradition says that when the family of a prospective groom brings the gift of Turkish delight to the potential bride's family, a sweet conversation will follow.

Sweets are usually eaten in the late afternoon as a social break in the day, with a cup of tea or a demitasse of dark Turkish coffee. Our friend Mahomet has been serving warm pistachio baklava in the afternoon for thirty years in his Konya *baklavaci* (baklava shop), like his father and grandfather before him. His profession is as honored today as it was a hundred years ago.

Muhallebi, or pudding, is a favorite dessert. In the Turkish kitchen, pudding is a traditional and beloved dish that lends itself to creative expression, as when it is spread atop caramel and rolled into a sumptuous roulade. Creamy baked rice pudding, with its golden brown skin, remains a comfort-food classic for many—us included.

And then there's rose milk pudding, fragrant pale pink and streaked with the occasional shred of petal. For five thousand years, roses have been cultivated and used as medicine, food and perfume in the Middle East, Persia and Turkey. The Greeks and Romans considered public gardens planted with fragrant *Rosa damascena* to be as important as grain. Today, Turkey is one of the leading producers of rose oil and rosewater. In Isparta, during harvest time, fields of pink roses transform the city with their scent.

Throughout Turkey, fruit—cherries served over ice in an elegant bowl, white peaches served whole, tart apple slices with honey or dried apricots stuffed with yogurt or thick cream—is preferred after an evening meal.

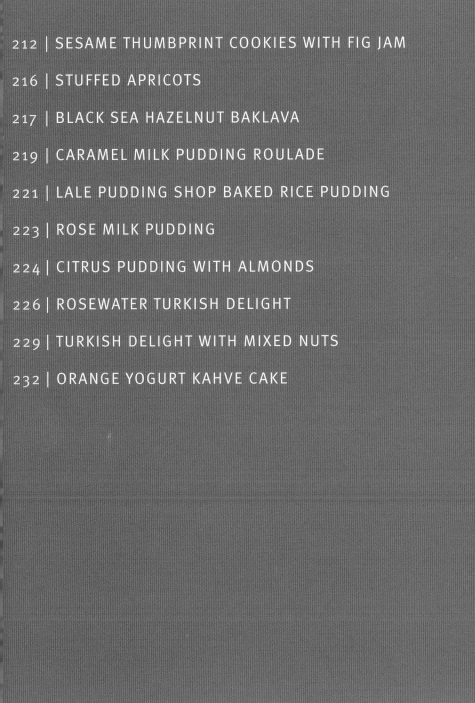

sesame thumbprint cookies with fig jam

MAKES 36 COOKIES

1 cup (450 g / 2 sticks) butter

½ cup (110 g) packed light brown sugar

2 large eggs

½ teaspoon pure vanilla extract

1 tablespoon orange zest

2½ cups (315 g) all-purpose flour

½ teaspoon kosher salt

1 cup (150 g) sesame seeds

⅓ cup (103 g) fig jam

Buttery thumbprint cookies, with their nut-studded exteriors and delicious jam centers, have been a part of our baking vocabulary since childhood. Here, we've introduced the flavors of the Levant—orange in the dough, sesame seeds for coating and a luscious fig jam filling—for a worldly take on a classic American cookie. Serve these as part of a dessert tray with Turkish delight and coffee, or as a sweet addition to breakfast.

Heat the oven to 350°F (175°C) and line 2 baking sheets with parchment.

In a medium mixing bowl, cream together the butter and brown sugar until light and fluffy, 2 to 3 minutes.

Separate the egg yolks from the whites, and set the egg whites aside. Add the yolks to the butter mixture 1 at a time, mixing well after each addition. Stir in the vanilla and the orange zest.

In a separate bowl, sift together the flour and salt. Combine the wet and dry ingredients and stir to create a firm dough.

In a small bowl, lightly beat the egg whites until frothy. Pour the sesame seeds onto a small plate and set it next to the bowl of egg whites.

To make the cookies, shape 2 teaspoons of dough into a ball. Roll it in the egg whites and then in the sesame seeds and set on the prepared baking sheet. Repeat with the remaining dough, placing the cookies about 1 inch (25 mm) apart.

With your thumb, make an indentation in each cookie. Lightly fill the indentation with ¼ to ½ teaspoon fig jam. Do not overfill.

Bake for 15 to 20 minutes, until the cookies are a delicate golden brown and slightly puffy. If the cookies begin browning too fast, lay a piece of parchment over the top for the last 5 minutes of baking.

Store the cookies in a tightly sealed container for 3 days, in the refrigerator for 1 week or in the freezer up to 1 month.

A SWEET TRIP TO THE BLACK SEA

On a late November day when the air held a hint of winter, Angie and her friend Sami drove from Istanbul up the Bosporus, east along the coast past lush dark pine forests to the seaside town of Ağva.

Sami, a bit of an epicure, was always surprising Angie with Anatolian delicacies. This time, he parked the car in front of a nut roaster and bakery for a taste of "special Black Sea baklava." Inside, the wood-fired oven gave welcome relief from the chill wind. Burlap bags filled with raw hazelnuts lined a wall next to racks containing trays of freshly roasted nuts. "The Black Sea region is where all the *fındıks* (hazelnuts) in Turkey are grown," explained Sami.

The shopkeeper turned toward a rack filled with trays of freshly baked baklava, sheets of toasty pillows cut into diamond, round, and square patterns still hot to the touch. Sami bought a dozen pieces. The shopkeeper poured sugar syrup, which sizzled in the pan as the pastry greedily soaked up the sweet liquid.

"We can never eat that many," Angie remembers saying.

With their fingers, they plucked squares from the box. Layers of buttery pastry and finely chopped hazelnuts seemed to evaporate on their tongues. Yes, the baklava was sweet, but not overly so. They ate another piece, and another. By the time they reached the highway back to Istanbul, the box was empty.

stuffed apricots
(ÇÜN KURUSU)

Delicate ripe apricots, just harvested in an orchard in Cappadocia

6 fresh apricots, peeled, pitted
    and cut in half, or 6 best-quality
    dried apricots
¼ to ½ cup (60 to 120 ml) Greek
    yogurt
2 tablespoons honey
2 tablespoons ground walnuts,
    pistachios or hazelnuts

SERVES 6

While rich sweets such as baklavas and puddings are usually enjoyed in the late afternoon with a cup of tea or coffee, Turks prefer fresh ripe fruit after the evening meal. The most prized apricots are those grown in the Malatya province, in rich alluvial soil from the Euphrates. Serving them with thick yogurt and local honey is typically Turkish. Add a sprinkling of ground, toasted nuts and serve for dessert or breakfast.

If using dried apricots, place them in bowl and cover with hot water. Soak for 20 minutes. Drain and pat dry on a paper towel.

Cut the apricots in half and lay them, cut side up, on a serving plate.

Stir the yogurt until smooth, and place a heaping ½ teaspoon on top of each apricot half. Drizzle the honey over the yogurt. Sprinkle with the ground nuts.

Black sea Hazelnut baklava

MAKES ABOUT 30 (1½-inch / 38 mm) PIECES

If you try tracing the origins of baklava, you will surely get lost, not only in time, but in place as well. Nearly every culture from Central Asia to Europe has a recipe for thin dough layered with sweetened nuts.

Turkey is the largest supplier of hazelnuts, producing 80 percent of the world's supply. And while nuts feature prominently in many Turkish dishes, hazelnuts reign supreme, lending their rich flavor to all manner of foods, especially sweets. An equal weight of unsalted shelled pistachios may be substituted for the hazelnuts. Today, Gaziantep, in the pistachio-growing region of southeastern Turkey, is famous for its crisp, not-too-sweet baklava.

To impress your guests, bake the baklava while having lunch or dinner. Remove it from the oven, and just before serving, bring the pan to the table. Pour the cool syrup over the hot pastry and listen to it sizzle as it releases a sweet, nutty aroma.

¾ pound (340 g) hazelnuts

¼ cup sugar

1 cup (450 g /2 sticks) butter

½ pound (227 g) filo dough

1 teaspoon lemon juice

Heat the oven to 275°F (135°C). Put the nuts in a single layer on a baking sheet and roast them in the oven for 15 to 30 minutes or until the skins crack and the nuts turn a light golden color.

Remove the nuts from the oven and put them in a clean kitchen towel. Let them cool for 10 minutes then rub vigorously in the towel to remove as much skin as possible.

Increase the oven temperature to 350°F (175°C). Put the roasted nuts in a food processor and pulse into a medium-fine grind, being careful not to process into a paste. Add ¼ cup of the sugar and pulse to blend. Reserve 1 tablespoon of the hazelnut-sugar mixture for finishing the baklava.

Melt the butter in a small saucepan. Using a pastry brush, coat the bottom of a 9 by 13-inch (23 by 33-cm) baking dish with a layer of butter. Place a sheet

(RECIPE CONTINUES)

217

Pistachio baklava beckons from a shop window in the southeastern city of Gazientep.

of filo dough over the butter. Brush another layer of butter over the filo and repeat until half of the filo sheets have been layered with butter. Brush the top piece of filo with butter. Keep the remaining dough covered with a damp kitchen towel to prevent it from drying out.

Sprinkle the hazelnut mixture evenly over the filo, pressing down gently to create an even surface. Continue to layer the remaining filo and butter over the nuts until all the filo sheets have been used. End with a final brushing of butter. Press down again gently on the surface of the pastry.

With a sharp knife, cut through the pastry on the diagonal beginning in 1 corner of the pan and cutting every 1½ to 2 inches (38 to 50 mm). Turn the pan around and make opposing cuts to create about 30 diamond-shaped pieces. (The baklava may be assembled up to a day in advance at this point, then covered tightly and refrigerated. Return to room temperature before baking.)

Put the baklava on the middle rack of the oven and bake for 15 to 20 minutes. Reduce the temperature to 300°F (149°C) and bake for 15 to 25 minutes more. The baklava should be lightly browned and crisp.

Meanwhile, make the syrup. Combine the remaining 1 cup (200 g) of sugar and ¾ cup (177 ml) water in a small pan over medium heat. When the syrup reaches a boil, reduce the heat and simmer for 5 minutes. Add the lemon juice and simmer for about 5 minutes more. Remove from the heat and cool to room temperature.

Remove the baklava from the oven and immediately pour the syrup evenly over the top, letting it sizzle and soak into the pastry. To finish, sprinkle the tablespoon of reserved hazelnut-sugar mixture over the pastry. Let the baklava rest for about 1 hour, and cut again to loosen each piece.

Serve the baklava at room temperature with Turkish coffee, mint tea and small glasses of water.

caramel milk pudding roulade (*kazandibi*)

SERVES 6 TO 8

along with Turkish Delight (page 228), *Kazandibi ve Tavuk Göğsü*, a rolled milk pudding with finely shredded chicken breast and a caramelized sugar crust, is a famous sweet to emerge from the kitchens of Ottoman court. You will find trays of kazandibi in the windows of every sweet shop, particularly in Istanbul. The concept of adding chicken to a sweet dessert is foreign to our tastes, so with the help of a friend, we've created this elegant version, which omits the chicken. It's another festive dessert that just happens to be gluten-free.

FOR THE CARAMEL

1 tablespoon butter, softened
½ cup (65 g) confectioner's sugar

FOR THE PUDDING

½ cup (65 g) cornstarch
½ cup (60 g) rice flour
1½ cups (354 ml) cold water
4¾ cups (11 dL) milk
1 cup (200 g) sugar
1 teaspoon pure vanilla extract
1 cup (130 g) finely ground unsalted pistachios
1 tablespoon cinnamon

FOR THE WHIPPED CREAM

1 cup (236 ml) heavy cream
1 teaspoon sugar
¼ teaspoon pure vanilla extract

1 pint (250 g) raspberries

MAKE THE CARAMEL LAYER: Lightly coat a 9 by 13-inch (23 by 33-cm) baking dish or quarter sheet pan with the butter. With a sieve, evenly sprinkle the confectioner's sugar over the butter. Turn a burner on the stove to medium-high. Wearing oven mitts and starting at the upper left hand corner of the pan, place it on the burner. Allow the butter and sugar to melt and bubble for about 30 seconds. Carefully continue rotating the pan until all the sugar has melted and the mixture turns deep golden brown. Make sure the caramel is evenly distributed over the bottom of the pan. Set aside.

MAKE THE PUDDING: In a small bowl, combine the cornstarch and the rice flour. Whisk in the cold water until the mixture is smooth. Set aside.

In a medium heavy saucepan over medium-high heat, combine the milk, sugar and vanilla, stirring to dissolve the sugar. As soon as the mixture comes to a boil, reduce the heat to medium.

Give the cornstarch-rice flour mixture a quick whisk and add it in a slow, steady stream to the milk mixture. Stir constantly for 3 to 4 minutes until the pudding becomes thick enough to spread. Remove from the heat.

Immediately spoon the warm pudding over the caramel, beginning in the

(RECIPE CONTINUES)

An array of milk-based desserts at a pudding shop on Divanyolu in Sultanahmet

center of the pan. Using an offset spatula, spread the pudding evenly outward over the caramel to the edges of the pan. Cool the pudding on a rack for about 1 hour. Refrigerate for 1 to 2 hours until firm, and up to 24 hours.

FINISH THE ROULADE: Sprinkle the pistachios evenly over the pudding. Gently lift the pudding along the long end of the pan and roll it over the pistachios. Keep rolling the pudding until it reaches the opposite end. Slide the roulade gently to the center of the pan. Spoon any leftover caramel over the roulade. With a fine-mesh sieve, sift the cinnamon over the roulade.

Make the whipped cream: Just before serving, pour the cream into a chilled bowl. With a wire whisk or electric hand mixer, whip the cream until it begins to thicken. Add the sugar and vanilla and whisk until soft peaks form.

Cut the roulade into 1½-inch (38-mm) pieces. Place 1 or 2 pieces on each serving plate, garnish with the raspberries and top with whipped cream.

Lale pudding shop baked rice pudding (fırın sütlaç)

SERVES 6

The Lale (tulip) Restaurant, better known as the Pudding Shop, became famous in the 1960s and 1970s as a meeting place for young people heading overland to India and Asia on what was known as the "hippie trail." In 1978 it was featured in the film *Midnight Express*. On a bulletin board set up by the owners, backpackers left notes for one another and waited for friends to arrive from far-flung locations, sitting in booths or in the garden eating inexpensive, filling rice pudding. Whenever we travel to Istanbul, we make a pilgrimage to the Pudding Shop for this ultimate comfort food. With its golden crust and creamy interior, it will please any child or adult.

¼ cup (30 g) cornstarch
4¾ cups (11 dL) milk, divided
½ cup (100 g) short-grain white rice
½ cup (100 g) suger
1 teaspoon pure vanilla extract

Heat the oven to 400°F (204°C). Put the cornstarch in a small bowl and add ¼ cup (60 ml) of the milk. Stir to create a slurry and set aside.

In a large saucepan combine the rice and enough water to cover by ½ inch (13 mm). Bring to a boil over medium heat. Reduce the heat and simmer for 5 minutes or until all the water has been absorbed.

Stir the remaining 4½ cups (11 dL) milk and the sugar into the rice. Set over medium-high heat and stir to dissolve the sugar. Bring to a boil, then reduce the heat and simmer for 20 minutes, stirring occasionally to prevent it from sticking to the bottom of the pan. The pudding will begin to thicken.

Remove ½ cup (120 ml) of the hot pudding and stir it into the cornstarch slurry. Pour the mixture back into the pot in a slow steady stream, stirring constantly. Add the vanilla and return the pudding to a low simmer. Cook without stirring for 2 minutes. The pudding will be thick.

Using a ladle, spoon the pudding into a 1½ quart (14 dL) baking dish or divide among individual 1-cup (236-ml) ramekins. Set in a baking pan with high sides and pour water ½ inch (13 mm) up the side of the baking dish or ramekins before sliding

(RECIPE CONTINUES)

BANJO JO—Couldn't wait any longer. Gone to Katmandu.
Love, Sylvie
—Sign on the bulletin board at the Lale Pudding Shop, circa 1960s

Warm, creamy milk pudding with pistachios is traditional Turkish comfort food.

the pan into the oven.

Bake for 30 to 35 minutes, until a deep brown skin forms on the top of the pudding. Remove from the oven, cool to room temperature and serve, or refrigerate the cooled pudding, covered, for up to 8 hours before serving.

ROSE MILK PUDDING

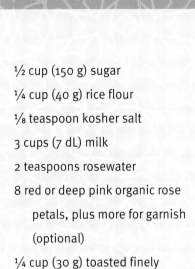

SERVES 4 TO 6

In Anatolia, Persia and the Middle East, *Rosa damascena*, the legendary Damascus rose, lends its fragrance to many dishes, including this elegant pudding. We first tasted it on a summer night in Istanbul on the balcony of Tugra Restaurant at the Çırağan Palace. A full moon was rising over the Bosporus when a waiter arrived with silver domed plates and set them before us. With a flourish, he removed the domes to reveal stemmed crystal glasses containing creamy custard garnished with deep red rose petals. We swooned at first bite and rushed to buy bottles of rosewater at the spice bazaar so we could recreate the pudding at home. These days we can easily find it in specialty shops, and this pudding has become a favorite among family and friends.

½ cup (150 g) sugar

¼ cup (40 g) rice flour

⅛ teaspoon kosher salt

3 cups (7 dL) milk

2 teaspoons rosewater

8 red or deep pink organic rose petals, plus more for garnish (optional)

¼ cup (30 g) toasted finely chopped pistachios

In a small bowl, combine the sugar, flour and salt.

In a medium heavy saucepan over moderate heat, combine the milk and the rosewater. Add the 8 rose petals, if using, along with the sugar mixture and whisk to combine.

Bring the pudding to a boil. Reduce the heat to simmer and cook, stirring constantly, until the mixture thickens and coats the spoon. This will take about 20 to 25 minutes. The rose petals will give up their color and should dissolve into the pudding. If desired, it can be strained before serving to remove any stray bits of flower petal.

Divide the pudding among serving bowls. Serve at room temperature, or let cool, cover and refrigerate for 1 hour or overnight. Before serving, garnish with the chopped pistachios and a reserved rose petal.

CITRUS PUDDING WITH ALMONDS

SERVES 4 TO 6

¼ cup (60 ml) cold water

¼ cup (30 g) cornstarch

1 grapefruit

1 Valencia or navel orange

1 cup (236 ml) orange juice, strained of pulp

1 cup (236 ml) grapefruit juice, strained of pulp

¾ cup plus 1 tablespoon (166 g) sugar

¾ cup (85 g) slivered almonds, 2 tablespoons reserved for garnish

1 cup (240 ml) whipped cream, for serving

½ cup (75 g) pomegranate seeds, for serving

Dessert and fruit are often served as separate courses at a Turkish dinner. Inspired by a recipe from an old Ottoman cookbook, we've combined them in this light but deeply flavored dessert that highlights tart and sweet citrus as well as fragrant almonds. We've modified the original by garnishing with whipped cream and jewel-like pomegranate seeds.

In a small bowl, whisk together the water and cornstarch until smooth.

Cut the grapefruit and the orange into supremes (see Note). Cut the supremes into bite-sized pieces and measure out a generous ½ cup each of the orange (85 g) and grapefruit (115 g). Set the fruit aside.

Pour the grapefruit and orange juices into a saucepan. Set over medium heat and add the sugar and the cornstarch mixture. Stir continuously until the mixture begins to turn clear and bubbles and thickens.

Add the grapefruit and orange supremes. Cook, stirring gently, for 2 minutes. Remove from the heat. Stir in the almonds and pour into individual serving dishes. Cool to room temperature, then cover and refrigerate for up to 8 hours.

Top with a dollop of sweetened whipped cream before serving. Garnish with the remaining almonds and pomegranate seeds.

Note: To supreme citrus, use a sharp knife to cut off the top and bottom of the fruit. Remove the peel and the pith following the curve of the peel down to the cutting board. To release the segments from their membranes, slide the knife between the segments and their membranes and cut the flesh away. Gently release each segment onto the cutting board. When finished, squeeze any remaining juice from the membranes and discard.

Rosewater Turkish Delight

Pistachios provide an earthy balance to floral rosewater, while cardamom in the confectioner's sugar coating adds a subtle warm flavor.

FOR THE SYRUP

2 cups (473 ml) cold water

2 cups (400 g) sugar

1 tablespoon lemon juice

2 tablespoons rosewater

Zest of 1 lemon

¼ teaspoon kosher salt

FOR THE NOUGAT

½ cup plus 2 tablespoons (75 g)
   cornstarch

½ teaspoon cream of tartar

1 cup (236 ml) cold water

1 tablespoon rosewater

2 drops natural red food color
   (optional)

1 cup (130 g) roasted, unsalted
   shelled pistachios

FOR THE SUGAR COATING

1 cup (125 g) confectioner's sugar

1 tablespoon ground cardamom

¾ cup (96 g) cornstarch

Spray an 8 by 8-inch (20 by 20-cm) square pan lightly with natural nonstick spray and dust it with cornstarch. Alternately, line the pan with parchment and dust the paper with cornstarch.

MAKE THE SYRUP: In a heavy saucepan, combine the cold water, sugar, lemon juice, rosewater, lemon zest and salt. If using a candy thermometer, clip it on the pan. Bring the mixture to a boil over high heat, stirring until the sugar dissolves. Reduce the heat to medium. Simmer for 30 minutes, stirring occasionally, to create a pale yellow syrup. Continue simmering for another 3 to 5 minutes until the surface is covered in bubbles or a candy thermometer reaches 260°F (127°C). Remove from the heat.

MAKE THE NOUGAT: In another heavy saucepan large enough to hold both the nougat and the syrup, combine the cornstarch, cream of tartar, 1 cup (236 ml) cold water and rosewater. Mix until smooth.

Put the saucepan over medium heat, and in a slow, steady stream, pour in the sugar syrup, stirring to combine. Cook for about 15 minutes, stirring constantly to prevent the mixture from sticking to the bottom of the pan, until it thickens and becomes a glossy nougat.

Remove from the heat. Add 2 drops of natural red food color, if desired. Add the pistachios and mix to combine. When the mixture is cool enough to handle, spread the nougat into the prepared pan. With oiled fingers, pat it to create a uniform flat surface about ¾-inch (19-mm) thick. It's okay if the nougat doesn't completely fill the pan. Allow the nougat to set at room temperature for 2 hours, or up to 12 hours.

MAKE THE SUGAR COATING: In a small bowl, combine the confectioner's

Bountiful display of Turkish Delight (lokum) and other sweets at the Egyptian spice bazaar in Istanbul

sugar, cardamom and cornstarch. Sift the mixture evenly onto a clean, dry work surface or a piece of parchment.

Carefully turn the nougat in a single piece onto the sugar coating. Oil a sharp knife with neutral vegetable oil and cut the nougat into 1-inch (25-mm) cubes. Turn the pieces to liberally coat them in the sugar.

Store the Turkish delight between layers of wax paper and loosely place a paper towel over the nougat before sealing in an airtight container. The paper towel will absorb excess moisture. The nougat will keep in the refrigerator for up to 2 months. Bring to room temperature, and, if necessary, roll again in powdered sugar before serving.

Haci Bekir, Istanbul's iconic sweet shop and purveyor of Turkish delight since 1777.

TURKISH DELIGHT

The shimmering treat known as Turkish delight has spawned imitators in every culture but was perfected in eighteenth-century Istanbul by a confectioner named Hacı Bekir. His rose, orange and pistachio-flavored confections gained the admiration of Sultan Mahmud II, who appointed him *helvacibasi*, or chief confectioner, at Topkapı Palace.

In Turkey, the Middle East, Russia, Greece and the Balkans, Turkish delight goes by the name *rahat lokum*, Arabic for comfortable or throat-soothing morsel, so called because in a hot and dusty landscape, a sugar-based candy with its humectant properties will soothe a dry or sore throat.

In the nineteenth century, an Englishman who, like many travelers before him, fell in love with Istanbul and its hurly-burly streets, discovered rahat lokum in Hacı Bekir's shop hidden in one of the twisty streets between Topkapı Palace and the Bosporus. The Englishman so loved rahat lokum that when he shipped a case back to London, he gave it a new name, Turkish delight. The jellied sweet captivated Londoners and novelists and soon found its way into trendy households from Paris to Moscow.

Our trips to Istanbul would not be complete without a stop at Hacı Bekir's famous sweet shop. Still owned by Bekir's descendants, the original can be found in Sultanahmet on the European side of the Bosporus. From Topkapı Palace, it's a pleasant walk down narrow streets that lead to the ferry docks at Eminönü. In the window of the shop on Hamidye Street, squares of Turkish delight shimmer in pale shades of rose, orange and yellow, piled high on ornate silver trays. The moment you open the door, you are enveloped in warmth and the sweet perfume of sugar.

turkish delight with mixed nuts

MAKES ABOUT 70 (1-INCH / 25-MM) SQUARES

Generous handfuls of toasted nuts take the classic citrus-scented nougat to another level. Traditionally, Turkish delight is flavored with rosewater. Our nut-rich version is a sophisticated alternative that's reminiscent of Italian and Spanish *torrone*. The nut mixture can be prepared a day or two ahead and stored in an airtight container.

Spray an 8 by 8-inch (20 by 20-cm) square pan lightly with natural nonstick spray and dust it with cornstarch. Alternately, line the pan with parchment and dust the paper with cornstarch.

TOAST THE NUTS (page 206): If the hazelnuts still have their skins, let them cool. When cool enough to handle, remove as much of the skin as possible by rubbing the hazelnuts in a clean kitchen towel.

MAKE THE SYRUP: In a medium heavy saucepan, combine the cold water, brown sugar, lemon juice, orange extract, zest, salt and mint leaves. If using a candy thermometer, clip it on the pan. Bring to a boil over high heat, stirring until the sugar dissolves. When the mixture boils, reduce the heat to medium-low and simmer for 30 minutes, stirring occasionally. The syrup should turn a rich dark brown. When bubbles cover the surface or the syrup reaches 260°F (127°C) on a candy thermometer, remove from the heat.

MAKE THE NOUGAT: While syrup simmers, in another heavy saucepan large enough to hold both the nougat and the syrup, combine the cornstarch, cream of tartar and cold water. Place over medium heat, stirring until perfectly smooth. In a slow steady stream, stir in the hot syrup. Cook for about 15 minutes, stirring constantly to prevent the nougat from sticking to the bottom of the pan. The mixture will become thick and glossy.

Scrape the nougat into a mixing bowl. Add the toasted walnuts, pistachios

(RECIPE CONTINUES)

FOR THE NUT MIXTURE
½ cup (60 g) walnuts, broken into
　　large pieces
½ cup (65 g) unsalted shelled
　　pistachios
½ cup (55 g) chopped hazelnuts

FOR THE SYRUP
2 cups (473 ml) cold water
2 cups (440 g) firmly packed light
　　brown sugar
1 tablespoon lemon juice
1 tablespoon orange extract
Grated zest of 1 orange or lemon
¼ teaspoon kosher salt
2 mint leaves

FOR THE NOUGAT
½ cup plus 2 tablespoons (75 g)
　　cornstarch
½ teaspoon cream of tartar
1 cup (236 ml) cold water

FOR THE SUGAR COATING
1 cup (125 g) confectioner's sugar
1 tablespoon ground cardamom
¾ cup (95 g) cornstarch

and hazelnuts, stirring until the mixture cools and the nuts are evenly distributed.

Spread the nougat into the prepared pan. With oiled fingers, press the nougat evenly into the pan to create as uniform a surface as possible. Allow the nougat to set at room temperature for at least 12 hours, or a total of 24 hours.

MAKE THE SUGAR COATING: In a small bowl, combine the confectioner's sugar, cardamom and cornstarch. Sift evenly onto a clean piece of parchment.

Carefully turn the nougat in a single piece onto the sugar coating. Oil a

Sifting a fresh batch of Turkish delight with powdered sugar and cornstarch

HONEY IN AN APPLE ORCHARD

A few years ago, on the eastern spur of the Silk Road, our rental car, a tiny Czech Škoda, broke down on a deserted stretch of road. As far as we knew, except for the whirr of cicadas chirring in the trees, we were the only living creatures in eastern Anatolia.

We had, however, seen a farmhouse about a mile behind us, and near it a man working in an apple orchard. Our dread easing, we set out for help.

By the time we reached the farmhouse, the man was standing on the porch, almost smiling as he took in the spectacle of two Western women loping toward him. After we explained our situation in broken Turkish, he beckoned us up wooden steps and through a heavy door into a small kitchen where a half fridge, propane stove and chipped porcelain sink were set into a counter beneath a window that looked out to the road. His wife was at the sink wearing a red cotton headscarf patterned with blue and yellow flowers and voluminous shalwar pants pleated at her ankles.

"*Hosgeldiniz*, welcome," she said, smiling as if she had been expecting us. From a red plastic bowl on the table, she withdrew a yellow apple, its skin flecked with copper.

sharp knife with neutral vegetable oil and cut the nougat into 1-inch (25-mm) cubes cubes. Turn the pieces to liberally coat them in the sugar.

Store the Turkish delight between layers of wax paper and loosely place a paper towel over the nougat to absorb excess moisture before sealing in an air-tight container. The nougat will keep in the refrigerator for up to 2 months, or in the freezer for 6 months. Bring to room temperature before serving.

While the man spoke quietly, she sliced the apple and arranged it on a plastic plate. After setting the plate and a jar of honey on the table, she shooed her husband down the steps toward the road.

"*Benim arkadaşlarim*, my friends," she said, and dipped apple slices into the honey, handing them to us. A second apple had been cut by the time the man returned, clucking his tongue and looking as if one of our closest relatives had died.

The Škoda was "kaput," as he said. We would have to wait for a tow truck.

The woman made tea and produced a small album containing photos of her daughter and grandchild. We had just finished our tea when, through the window, we saw that our Škoda had been secured on a flatbed truck that idled on the side of the road, its red cab swirled with yellow and white flowers.

The woman noticed our distress and into our backpacks went more golden apples. Touching her hand to her heart, she said, "*Herşey güzel olacak.*" All will be well, indeed.

orange yogurt kahve cake

MAKES 1 (9-inch / 23-cm) CAKE, SERVING 8 TO 10

When our northern and eastern European families left their homelands for new lives working on farms and in factories in the American Midwest, they brought their languages and traditions—and traditional recipes for sour cream coffee cake. As children, we loved the coffee klatches where our mothers, aunts, grandmothers and neighbors gathered to gossip over slices of moist, nutty cake accompanied by cups of coffee poured straight from the percolator. Sometimes, if we were lucky, they'd allow us a cup with a lot of milk.

Kahve means coffee in Turkish. So, with nostalgia and the addition of typically Anatolian yogurt, cardamom and orange, we've melded cultures just as immigrants have always done in this easy-to-love cake that's just made for socializing.

Heat the oven to 350°F (175°C). Lightly grease a 9-inch (23-cm) tube or Bundt cake pan with oil, making certain to oil the tube section as well.

MAKE THE STREUSEL: In a small bowl, combine the brown sugar, flour, cinnamon, cardamom and orange zest. Cut the butter into 6 pieces. With a fork or pastry cutter, incorporate the butter into the sugar mixture until the streusel sticks together when pinched with your fingers. Stir in the chopped walnuts and set aside.

MAKE THE CAKE BATTER: In a medium bowl, whisk together the flour, baking powder, baking soda and salt. In a larger mixing bowl, or the bowl of an electric stand mixer, cream the butter until smooth and fluffy, about 3 minutes. Add the sugar and mix for 2 to 3 more minutes, frequently scraping the sides of the bowl. Add the eggs 1 at a time, incorporating each egg before adding the next. Add the flour mixture a little at a time until fully absorbed into the egg mixture. Stir in the orange juice and the yogurt.

Vegetable oil, for greasing the pan

FOR THE STREUSEL

¼ cup (55 g) packed brown sugar

½ cup (65 g) all-purpose flour

1 teaspoon cinnamon

½ teaspoon ground cardamom

1 teaspoon grated orange zest

3 tablespoons butter

¾ cup (90 g) chopped walnuts

FOR THE CAKE

2½ cups (315 g) all-purpose flour

2 teaspoons baking powder

½ teaspoon baking soda

½ teaspoon kosher salt

¾ cup (170 g / 1½ sticks) butter, at room temperature

1 cup (200 g) sugar

3 large eggs

1 tablespoon orange juice

1¼ cups (200 ml) Greek yogurt

FOR THE GLAZE

½ cup (65 g) confectioner's sugar

½ teaspoon orange extract, or 1 teaspoon pure vanilla extract

1 to 4 teaspoons milk, as needed

Spread a third of the batter evenly over the bottom of the prepared cake pan. Sprinkle half of the streusel mixture over the batter. Repeat with another third of the batter, covering the streusel completely, and sprinkle with remaining streusel mixture. Finish with the remaining batter.

Set the cake on the center rack of the oven. Bake 50 to 60 minutes until a skewer inserted in the cake comes out clean. Set on a rack and let it cool in the pan for at least 30 minutes.

Before removing the cake, use a thin, sharp knife to cut along the outside edge of the cake and the center of the tube. If using an angel food cake pan, pull out the center tube and carefully slide the knife between the cake and the pan to help release the cake. Carefully invert the cake onto a serving plate.

MAKE THE GLAZE: Sift the confectioner's sugar into a small bowl. Add the orange extract and 1 teaspoon milk. Stir to blend. Continue adding milk, 1 teaspoon at a time, until the glaze becomes a thin, opaque frosting. With a spoon, drizzle the glaze in crisscross ribbons over the cake, letting it stream down the sides.

Serve warm or at room temperature with afternoon tea or Turkish coffee, or as a sweet addition to breakfast or brunch.

CHAPTER 12

BREWED BEVERAGES AND FESTIVE DRINKS

BY THE TIME THE WISE WOMAN HAS FOUND THE BRIDGE,
THE CRAZY WOMAN HAS CROSSED THE WATER.
— *TURKISH PROVERB*

coffee, tea AND RAKI

Afternoon tea and conversation at a neighborhood café in Izmir, on the Aegean coast

tea (*çay*), the most popular drink in Turkey, might also be its universal symbol of hospitality. In the late 1930s, the newly formed Republic sought a replacement for expensive imported coffee. Seventy tons of black tea seeds were bought from neighboring Georgia and planted along the eastern edge of the Black Sea in the plateaus of Rize Province where the vibrant green plants thrive in the temperate, moist climate and rich soil. Today, Turkey is the fifth-largest producer of tea and its fourth-largest consumer.

Turkey's first coffee house was opened in Istanbul in 1555 by two Syrian traders, but the art of coffee preparation and drinking coffee in Turkey was perfected by Sufi practitioners who relied on coffee's stimulating properties to stay awake during long periods of prayer. The drink soon became popular with intellectuals and was called "milk of chess players and thinkers." Cafés attracted writers, journalists, artists, musicians and poets, and even spawned book clubs.

Western visitors coveted an invitation to the ambassador's residence in Istanbul, where they would be served Black Pearl, the most prized coffee blend of its day. One French visitor, the seventeenth-century aristocrat Madame de Sévigné, observed that "Drinking coffee is a fad; it shall be forgotten one day." Still, she and her fellow visitors to Anatolia brought the taste for brewed coffee back home with them to Europe.

Between sunset and twilight, for those who drink alcohol, another tradition begins: the rakı *sofrası*, or rakı table, where friends gather to unwind, share small plates of food and drink icy glasses of anise-flavored rakı. Along with plates of melon, soft cheese, olives, eggplant puree and many other mezes, it is said that conversation should be your first meze.

turkish tea

Tea vendor at the Grand Bazaar in Istanbul with a tray full of hot çay

erved in small tulip-shaped glasses with sugar cubes on the side, çay is routinely offered in private homes, cafés, shops and restaurants. Many travelers avoid accepting tea from merchants, anticipating that once inside a shop, they will feel pressure to buy something. While this may indeed be the case, many of our fondest travel memories, best-loved treasures and oldest friendships are the result of saying yes to a cup of tea.

Traditional Turkish çay is prepared using a 2-part kettle or *çaydanlık*. The larger bottom kettle is filled with 6 cups (14 dL) of water for 6 servings. About ¼ cup (8 g) of loose tea is placed in the smaller kettle on top, and the whole kettle is placed over high heat. When the water in the bottom kettle comes to a boil, the host removes the top kettle and pours about half of the boiling water into it, then replaces the top kettle on the bottom kettle and sets the heat to low for 15 minutes to infuse the tea leaves and steep them into a very strong brew.

When the strong tea is served, it is traditionally poured into a cup that is filled halfway. It is further diluted with additional hot water from the bottom kettle, giving guests a choice among strong (*koyu*), medium (*tavşan kanı*) or light (*açık*) tea.

turkish coffee

Cezve, the classic Turkish coffee pots made of hammered copper

More expensive than tea, coffee is usually served with a sweet, such as baklava, and a glass of water for refreshment.

The traditional Turkish coffee pot is called a *cezve*. These beautiful small vessels made of brass or copper, sometimes etched with Ottoman designs, have a long wooden handle to protect the hands from the heat.

Properly brewed Turkish coffee has a thick, flavorful foam on top. The delicious, creamy foam acts as a protective layer, keeping the coffee warm. The coffee is prepared without a filter, and unlike drip coffee, is mixed directly with water. It must never come to a full boil.

To use a cezve to make 2 demitasse servings, combine 1 tablespoon ground coffee, ½ to 1 teaspoon of sugar per cup to taste (if desired) and 5 ounces (148 ml) of water in the pot and place over medium-high heat. Stir occasionally until the top of the coffee begins to foam up. Turn the heat down, or remove from the burner, and stir. Place over low heat without stirring until the top foams once more. Take off the heat before it reaches a boil and pour into demitasse cups, letting the grounds sink to the bottom. Serve immediately.

After finishing their coffee, Turks place the saucer over the cup and turn it upside down. They wait a few minutes before removing the cup to reveal a fortune in the pattern left by the coffee dregs.

turkish raki

1½ ounces (44 ml) Turkish rakı
1½ to 2 ounces (44 to 60 ml)
    filtered water
2 or 3 ice cubes

Dmitri lays a rug across my
      knees.
Wool cloth woven one hundred
      years before.
Red, lime, lemon, blue,
mountain, sky and sea.

From his desk,
he withdraws a glass, a bottle
of clear liquid. Rakı.

Firewater.

If you drink too much,
it will make you crazy,
you will lose your head.
But a little—
—J.E.S.

SERVES 1

Rakı is a decidedly acquired taste, but given the chance, we think it could become a regular aperitif in the States and elsewhere as it is in Turkey. A dry, anise-flavored alcoholic beverage, rakı is similar to Greek ouzo and French pastis, and it is served with mezes or as a late-night beverage at cafés where friends, old and new, gather.

The word *rakı* comes from the Arabic *araq*, meaning distilled. When mixed with ice and water, rakı turns a translucent moonstone color and is known as lion's milk, *aslan sütü*, because it is said that drinking it will make you as strong as a lion. You can find it in liquor stores, but if your local purveyor doesn't have it, they can easily order a bottle. Two of the most popular Turkish brands, Yeni and Efe, are often available in the States.

In Turkey, rakı is often served neat in the glass with a small dish of ice and a pitcher of water on the side so that each person can choose the strength of their drink.

Rakı is always paired with a selection of mezes such as Anatolian Nut Mix (page 18), Attila's Olives with Garlic and Preserved Lemons (page 14) Melon with Feta, Mint and Pomegranate (page 106), Eggplant Puree (page 26), Yogurt Dip with Cucumber and Mint (page 22) and Classic Puffed Pide Bread (page 62).

Pour the rakı into a 6- to 8-ounce (177- to 237-ml) glass. Pour the filtered water over it to taste. The rakı will begin to turn milky white. Gently stir with a small spoon, add 2 or 3 ice cubes and serve.

For a refreshing summer cocktail, replace plain water with a pitcher of water infused with cucumber and mint.

PERSEPHONE'S REVENGE

SERVES 1

2 ounces (60 ml) fresh-squeezed
   pomegranate juice

2 or 3 ice cubes

1½ ounces (44 ml) Turkish rakı

1 ounce (30 ml) water

2 or 3 pomegranate seeds
   (optional), for garnish

Wherever we walked in northern Cyprus, we found ripe yellow pomegranates hanging from trees. One afternoon we plucked a few from an abandoned orchard and brought them back to our guesthouse kitchen at the Gardens of Irini in Bellapais.

We were soon leaning over the kitchen counter, knives in hand, slicing open the pomegranates to reveal their gorgeous red seeds. We squeezed the fresh pomegranate juice by hand into glasses and, since it was cocktail time, decided to add rakı. A new drink was born.

Later in our journey, when we reached the Kelebek Hotel in Cappadocia, we shared our drink recipe with the owner. It wasn't long before the hotel manager brought us a bag of bright red pomegranates and we were put to work behind the bar.

We call it Persephone's Revenge in honor of the nymph Persephone, daughter of the goddess of grain, Demeter. As a young girl, Persephone was seduced by Hades, the god of the underworld, who tricked her into eating three pomegranate seeds. Having tasted the forbidden fruit, she was bound to spend a third of every year with Hades in the underworld. Since Persephone was the goddess of the spring and vegetation, her time spent in the underworld became winter, a time when no crops would grow.

To make the pomegranate juice, remove the jewel-like seeds from a ripe pomegranate and place them in a blender. Reserve a few seeds for garnish, if using. Pulse for 30 seconds to release the juice and put the seeds and juice into a metal sieve over a bowl. Press down on the seeds until all the juice is extracted. (You may also use store-bought pomegranate juice.)

Place 2 or 3 ice cubes in a small clear 6- to 8-ounce (177- to 237-ml) glass. Pour the rakı over the ice. The rakı will begin to turn milky white. Add the

Ripe and juicy, the golden pomegranates of Bellapais, in Cyprus, are a joy to pluck from the tree.

Pomegranate juice and water. Gently stir to combine. Add the pomegranate seeds, if using, letting them sink to the bottom.

BOSPORUS fizz

2 ounces (60 ml) rakı

2 ounces (60 ml) carrot juice

1 teaspoon turmeric

3 tablespoons Rosewater-Infused
    Simple Syrup (page 248) or
    Rose-Infused Simple Syrup with
    Fresh Rose Petals (page 249)

2 large ice cubes

4 ounces (120 ml) club soda

2 sprigs carrot greens, for garnish

SERVES 2

Our friend, mixologist Warren Bobrow, created this colorful cocktail, pairing rakı with fresh carrot juice and turmeric.

He tells us that turmeric, a natural anti-inflammatory and antioxidant, is thought to improve brain function and reduce arthritic pain, and according to Chinese medicine, it may be useful for easing depression. It's also reputed to be a powerful aphrodisiac. We know it adds a beautiful color to this stimulating drink.

Combine the rakı, carrot juice, turmeric and simple syrup in a cocktail shaker. Shake well until combined, about 20 seconds.

Place 1 ice cube each in 2 rocks or short glasses. Strain the carrot mixture into the glasses over the ice. Top off with the club soda and garnish with a tiny sprig of carrot greens.

ayran

SERVES 4 TO 6

4 cups (880 ml) plain yogurt

1½ cups (354 ml) ice water

1 to 2 teaspoons kosher salt

a classic refresher available everywhere in Turkey, ayran is a mixture of yogurt and water with a pinch of salt. Beneficial to the digestive system, this frothy drink is a cool counterpoint to spicy, fatty street foods like meat köfte, kebabs and lahmacun (Turkish pizza). While ayran is easy to make, today many Turkish restaurants and markets sell commercially produced ayran sold in sealed plastic cups.

Ayran "Bursa style," named for the region south of Istanbul in and around the city of Susurluk near Bursa, is served with an extra frothy head, like a yogurt latte. Ayran may also be made with fresh mint or fizzy mineral water, although we prefer this classic recipe.

In a 2-quart (19 dL) pitcher, whisk the yogurt until smooth. Slowly whisk in the water until frothy. (A handheld mixer or a blender may also be used.) Add 1 teaspoon of the salt and whisk to combine. Season to taste with more salt as desired. Serve immediately.

For an extracold drink, chill the glasses before serving or add a few ice cubes to your glass.

ROSEWATER-INFUSED SIMPLE SYRUP

the syrup improves in flavor if kept overnight in the refrigerator before using.

½ cup (100 g) sugar

1 tablespoon rosewater

In a small saucepan, combine the sugar with ½ cup (120 ml) water and set over medium-high heat. Stir until the sugar dissolves and the mixture begins to boil. Add the rosewater and bring back to a boil. Turn the heat down and simmer for 10 minutes. Set aside to cool.

Simple syrup will keep refrigerated in an airtight container for up to 1 month.

RETURN TO THE LYCIAN SEA

Bosporus blue light has given way to the diaphanous pearly mist of the Aegean countryside. We are on our way from Istanbul to Kalkan, with a stop at Ephesus.

Sprawled on cushions on the rooftop restaurant of our hotel in Selcuk, not far from the ruins of Ephesus, we drink coffee and savor the antics of a pair of black and white cats. They leap from a cinderblock wall in fruitless pursuit of a rose-colored canary, which taunts them from the safety of her cage beneath the eaves.

The sweet air hints at a sensuous unseen world of the feminine. In

Rose-infused simple syrup with fresh rose petals

Wrap the rose petals in a piece of cheesecloth and tie securely with a piece of kitchen twine.

Pour the simple syrup into a small bowl and submerge the cheesecloth bag into the syrup. Cover and store in the refrigerator overnight.

Remove the cheesecloth. Keep the syrup refrigerated in an airtight container for up to 1 month.

Note: Prepare the simple syrup following the recipe for Rosewater-Infused Simple Syrup but omit the rosewater. It can be used immediately, without overnight refrigeration.

6 organic red rose petals

1 cup (236 ml) simple syrup (see Note)

the east, remnants of the Anatolian mother goddess were hidden in caves, obscured in myth and buried under monasteries and mosques. In Ephesus, however, excavations continue within several acres of marble, rubble and dirt to reveal the high status of the goddess the Ephesians called Artemis.

After breakfast, we walk to the Selcuk Museum to see the statue of Artemis. On our way there, in the doorway of a timber and white stucco house, two women tie herbs into bunches and place them into a wicker basket.

acknowledgments

In Turkey: Istanbul Culinary Institute; Didem Şenol of Lokanta Maya, the chefs at Matbah, Asitane, Tuğra, and Ciya restaurants; Eveline Zoutendijk, the Women's Cooperative Restaurant in Avanos; Sakir Karaaslan, his sister, mother, aunts and extended family; Erguvanozgur Unal, Shellie Corman and Alper Ertube.

West Coast: Humyera and Rasim Konyar, Anne and James Hubbell, Pat Straube, owner of Orchard Hill; Anne Mery, owner of West Grove Collective; Carol Pike, Elisabeth Jacobsen, Heidi Schlotfeldt and Debra Palma; the staff and students at Spencer Valley School in Julian, California; David, Loretta and Jackson Brenner-Smith; Cathy Pettigrew and Joe De Francesco.

Midwest: Bezmi Krasnick, Aunt Mary Towne, Madonna Williams, Maureen Young Stallé and the members of their book clubs who were some of our very first tasters.

East Coast: Our Boston posse Caroline Gardner, Linnea Veigh, and Helen Shapiro. Also Sandra and Bob King, Barry Welch, Andrew and Rachel Kilmer, and chef Ana Sortun, whose menus at Oleana continue to inspire. New York: Our agent, Sarah Jane Freymann, the wonderful team at Burgess Lea Press, Andrew Smith, Lizet Gediciyan, Blue Guidal, Asya Graf, Jakab Orsos, Kalustyan's; Molyvos restaurant and Belgin's Turkish Kitchen. New Jersey: Fred and Sarah Young, Suzanne Perrault, sultana of gougères; Susan Sanchez-Murphy, William Wyman, Shelley Wiseman of the Farm Cooking School, chef John and Susanne Swizeny; chef and cocktail whisperer Warren Bobrow; Scott and Sandy Desch, Amy and John Constantine, Patti Mecca and Mark Nolan; Peter and Dorothy Stocke; and a special thanks to Kim Nagy and the team at Wild River. In Princeton, New Jersey: Dorothea von Moltke and Cliff Simms, literary and culinary angels; Edmund Keeley, Kathleen Crown, John and Christi Timpane, Landon Jones, Nell Whiting. In Philadelphia: Joyce Spindler and Shirley Powell-Cohen, connoisseurs of Turkish Delight; chef Owen Lee, owner of Park Plates; Emily Gallagher and Austin Elston of Born Lucky Studios.

Food photographs © Jason Varney. Other photographs: 12, 31, 41, 63, 90, 101, 119, 172, 210, 216, 220, 222, 238, 245 © Joy Stocke; 17, 29, 32, 38, 48, 51, 54, 59, 69, 80, 108, 114, 134, 142, 149, 152, 166, 184, 196, 218, 227, 228, 230, 236, 240 iStock/Getty Images; 6, 9, Shutterstock; 84, 85, 94, 169 © Alastair Campbell; 111 © Jumeirah International LLC.

INDEX